GLOBAL HISTORY OF THE PRESENT
Series editor | Nicholas Guyatt

In the Global History of the Present series, historians address the upheavals in world history since 1989, as we have lurched from the Cold War to the War on Terror. Each book considers the unique story of an individual country or region, refuting grandiose claims of 'the end of history', and linking local narratives to international developments.

Lively and accessible, these books are ideal introductions to the contemporary politics and history of a diverse range of countries. By bringing a historical perspective to recent debates and events, from democracy and terrorism to nationalism and globalization, the series challenges assumptions about the past and the present.

Published

Thabit A. J. Abdullah, *Dictatorship, Imperialism and Chaos: Iraq since 1989*

Timothy Cheek, *Living with Freedom: China since 1989*

Alexander Dawson, *First World Dreams: Mexico since 1989*

Padraic Kenney, *The Burdens of Freedom: Eastern Europe since 1989*

Stephen Lovell, *Destination in Doubt: Russia since 1989*

Forthcoming

Alejandra Bronfman, *On the Move: The Caribbean since 1989*

James D. Le Sueur, *Between Terror and Democracy: Algeria since 1989*

Mark LeVine, *Impossible Peace: Israel/Palestine since 1989*

Hyung Gu Lynn, *Bipolar Orders: The Two Koreas since 1989*

Nivedita Menon and Aditya Nigam, *Power and Contestation: India since 1989*

Helena Pohlandt-McCormick, *What Have We Done? South Africa since 1989*

Nicholas Guyatt is assistant professor of history at Simon Fraser University in Canada.

About the author

Padraic Kenney divides his time between Wrocław, Poland and the University of Colorado at Boulder, where he is professor of history. He is the author of several books on Eastern European history and politics, including *A Carnival of Revolution: Central Europe, 1989* (2002). His next book will examine the experience of political prisoners in twentieth-century world history.

The Burdens of Freedom: Eastern Europe since 1989

Padraic Kenney

Fernwood Publishing
NOVA SCOTIA

Zed Books
LONDON | NEW YORK

The Burdens of Freedom: Eastern Europe since 1989 was first published in 2006

Published in Canada by Fernwood Publishing Ltd, 32 Oceanvista Lane, Site 2A, Box 5, Black Point, Nova Scotia B0J 1B0

<www.fernwoodbooks.ca>

Published in the rest of the world by Zed Books Ltd, 7 Cynthia Street, London N1 9JF, UK and Room 400, 175 Fifth Avenue, New York, NY 10010, USA

<www.zedbooks.co.uk>

Copyright © Padraic Kenney, 2006

Cover designed by Andrew Corbett
Set in OurType Arnhem and Futura Bold by Ewan Smith, London
Index <ed.emery@britishlibrary.net>
Printed and bound in Malta by Gutenberg Press Ltd

Distributed in the USA exclusively by Palgrave Macmillan, a division of St Martin's Press, LLC, 175 Fifth Avenue, New York, NY 10010.

A catalogue record for this book is available from the British Library.
US CIP data are available from the Library of Congress.

Library and Archives Canada Cataloguing in Publication:
Kenney, Padraic, 1963-
    The burdens of freedom : Eastern Europe since 1989 / Padraic Kenney.
ISBN 1-55266-205-5
    1. Europe, Eastern--History--1989-. 2. Europe, Eastern--Politics and government--1989-. I. Title.
DJK51.K464 2006   947'.0009049   C2006-902638-6

ISBN   1 84277 662 2 | 978 1 84277 662 9 hb
ISBN   1 84277 663 0 | 978 1 84277 663 6 pb

Contents

Acknowledgments | vi

Maps | viii–ix

Introduction: the shock of the new | 1

1   Different paths on an open road: economic and
     social change | 15

2   In praise of ethnic cleansing? National struggles | 45

3   Peeling away the past: nostalgia and punishment | 75

4   Portraits of hubris: democratic politics | 100

5   A new Europe: the East in the West | 128

     Conclusion: the edge of history | 159

     Notes | 163

     Index | 171

Acknowledgments

The very existence of this book owes a great deal to series editor Nicholas Guyatt. His prompting led me to consider and accept the project, and he has been an extraordinarily thoughtful and helpful reader throughout. My colleagues Elizabeth Dunn and Jacek Lubecki, and my father Michael Kenney, also read drafts and offered excellent suggestions. Students in a seminar I taught in the International Affairs Program at Colorado in the spring of 2005 helped me to work out many of the ideas in this book. Thanks to all of you.

Much of this book took shape with a view of the Park Nowowiejski in Wrocław. It owes a great deal to colleagues, friends and family across Eastern Europe. I am grateful to my wife, Izabela, for her support and encouragement, and to Fredzio Zapałka and all his friends.

Eastern Europe in 1989

SWEDEN

FINLAND

Helsinki

Stockholm

Moscow

Baltic Sea

UNION OF SOVIET
SOCIALIST REPUBLICS

Copenhagen

DENMARK

Berlin

Warsaw

EAST
GERMANY

POLAND

Prague

WEST
GERMANY

CZECHOSLOVAKIA

Vienna

Budapest

AUSTRIA

HUNGARY

ROMANIA

Belgrade

Bucharest

Black Sea

YUGOSLAVIA

SAN
MARINO

ITALY

Sofia

BULGARIA

Adriatic Sea

Rome

VATICAN CITY

Tirana

ALBANIA

Ankara

TURKEY

GREECE

Ionian
Sea

Athens

0   km   400

Mediterranean   Sea

Map by **MAP**grafix

Eastern Europe in 2006

B-H	**BOSNIA-HERZEGOVINA**
K	**Kosovo**
MAC	**REPUBLIC OF MACEDONIA**
SL	**SLOVENIA**
R	**RUSSIA**
- - -	Boundaries new or changed since 1989

0   km   400

N

SWEDEN

FINLAND

RUSSIA

Helsinki

Stockholm   Tallinn
ESTONIA

Moscow

Riga
LATVIA

LITHUANIA
Copenhagen   Vilnius
DENMARK   **R**

Minsk

BELARUS

Berlin   Warsaw
POLAND

Kiev

GERMANY

UKRAINE

Prague
CZECH REPUBLIC   **SLOVAKIA**

MOLDOVA

Vienna   Bratislava
AUSTRIA   **HUNGARY**

Kishinev

Budapest

Ljubljana   Zagreb
SL   **CROATIA**

ROMANIA

Belgrade
SERBIA
B-H   **and**

Bucharest

Black Sea

SAN MARINO   Sarajevo
ITALY   **MONTENEGRO**

Sofia

Rome   **K**
VATICAN CITY   Tirana   Skopje
MAC   **BULGARIA**

Ankara

ALBANIA

GREECE

TURKEY

Baltic Sea

Adriatic Sea

Ionian Sea

Athens

Mediterranean Sea

Map by **MAP**grafix

Introduction: the shock of the new

Eastern Europe: what's in a name? One can start quite a debate over the proper terminology for the region that is the subject of this book. East-Central Europe, Central and Southeast (or Balkan?) Europe, West-Central Europe, *Mitteleuropa* ... Perhaps finding the right combination of terms makes no difference. Yet these can be fighting words, too. I first learned this in Moscow, in 1984. Sitting in a beer hall near our dormitory, I burbled enthusiastically to my Slovak friend Jano about a course I had taken at Harvard on East European literature. "East European literature – what could that be?" he wondered. Kundera! Kiš! Miłosz![1] I chattered on until he cut me off, somewhat grimly: "Czechoslovakia is Western Europe. Eastern Europe – that's India."

Jano's geography was clearly of the extreme variety. But any sharp-eared visitor to the region today will notice the same chill around the words "Eastern Europe" or "Balkan." They connote backwardness, or Russianness. "Central" is the preferred term – or, better yet, just "Europe."

Yet "Eastern" is unavoidable in this book, as a term to unite – what? The fifteen countries from Estonia to Macedonia that receive attention here share a few traits. All have definitively broken away not only from Soviet-style communism, but from the Russian sphere of influence, something that cannot yet be said about Ukraine, or Moldova, or Belarus. All have either joined the European Union, are slated to join within a year or two, or are at least considered potential candidates, with some hope of beginning membership negotiations someday. Of course, in other ways these fifteen have little in common, while the borders of the region are sometimes indistinct. The Czech Republic is much more like its neighbor Austria than it is like Albania; Lithuanians and Ukrainians have many common experiences that even a Pole born and raised under communism would find unfamiliar. But overall, the paths these fifteen are taking, and the difficulties they face, are quite similar economically, culturally, politically.

Now for another caveat: Fifteen countries, no matter how comparable, are a lot for a book of any length. Nor would it be interesting, even for the specialist, to follow each of them in detail, one after another, over nearly two decades of post-communism, whether in alphabetical or some other order. The approach in this book, then, is synecdochal: while there are very many interesting stories about every country, in this book a part must stand for the whole. The Lithuanian commemoration of communism may be as compelling as the Hungarian, or Czech corruption scandals as important as those in Albania, but one simply has to choose. To be clear, though: Choice is made not simply for brevity, but more because what is interesting are the overall trends, which are as well illustrated with one or two examples as with a dozen.

Too often, contemporary history ends up being simply a catalog of events, as if synthesis must wait until all the bodies are properly buried. Yet I decided to write this book because I realized, as the European Union enlarged into Eastern Europe on May 1, 2004, that a historical period had almost certainly come to an end. Often, turning points have a way of disappearing at a distance of just a few months. This time, it seems more and more certain that the post-communist era came to a close at that time. Other domestic and international events, to be discussed herein, seem to confirm the sense that a narrative arc can now be described across the seventeen years since 1989.

What is that narrative? First, there can be no doubt: Eastern Europe as a whole, and the vast majority of East Europeans themselves, are better off than they were before 1989. They enjoy greater civil and economic freedoms, have greater access to information and to both necessary and luxury goods, and are safer and more secure. This does not excuse the historian from exploring the failures of the post-communist era: the people neglected by the new economic system, or suffering greater repression than before, above all the millions killed, wounded, or driven from their homes in the former Yugoslavia since 1991. One must also consider the missed chances to avoid hardship, or to choose a still better way. The tragedies of the post-communist era – in particular the genocide in Bosnia and the ethnic cleansing there, in Croatia, and in Kosovo, but also the difficult crises that have struck most countries at one time or another – most certainly could have been avoided. But the pessimist will find little satisfaction in the history of post-communist Eastern Europe. One need not give up on the hope that humanity can find a better, fairer, or more moral way to conduct its affairs to recognize that, simply, life is better without the communists.

Of course, if one wants to find pessimists, there is no better place to look than Eastern Europe itself. Pangloss is a loner there. A Eurobarometer survey conducted on the eve of EU enlargement found nearly one-third of respondents in new member-states – as high as 41 percent in Slovakia – predicting their lives would be worse in the coming year; 39 percent expected their financial situation in particular to worsen. These totals were about twice as high as in the "old" member-states. Looking back, East Europeans were also much more likely to say life had worsened in the last five years.[2] Still, an honest look at the region's recent history leaves little doubt that most change has been for the better. As we shall see, there are plenty of reasons for nostalgia for the communist past, but the historian need not join in this chorus.

What exactly was wrong with the communist system? First, the system of central planning limited what society could accomplish. Movement between countries, or within them, was limited by the need to manage resources for the purpose of regime economic goals – as well as, of course, by fears of the spread of discontent. Especially in the first two decades after 1945, communist societies underwent massive social mobility, as peasants moved to the cities and acquired education, skilled jobs, and the accoutrements of modern living; workers, too, found that membership of the ruling party opened doors to higher education and to elite careers. Yet by the 1980s, the paths of rapid advancement were fewer, and the expectations of younger generations higher; lack of housing – in some cities, one had to wait between fifteen and twenty years for a small apartment – was just one of the factors limiting individual opportunity in late communism.

A second problem was the communist system's inability to adapt. Scholars are in general if grudging agreement that through the early 1970s growth rates and technological sophistication in the region did not differ radically from those in Western Europe. In terms of standards of living and access to consumer goods, the gap between East and West was greater, as communist economies devoted more of their efforts to heavy industry and less both to the production of consumer goods and (as anyone who has ever stood in line in an East European grocery can attest) to the development of retail outlets. Still, this gap was small enough that some scholars could envision a convergence between the different socio-economic systems. The combination of the oil shock and the development of the micro-processor buried such speculation. By 1980, the communist regimes were hopelessly behind. They had accumulated tens of billions of dollars in debt to Western governments and banks, were seeing their cherished industries turning obsolete, and had less and less to offer their citizens – who were, in turn, becoming aware (through television and radio, and through visits abroad) that people of the same class lived better elsewhere, and that the infrastructure of Western countries was vastly superior, too. While a few countries – primarily Yugoslavia, Hungary, and Poland – had either experimented with market hybrids or some forms of private ownership, all without exception were merely hobbling along by the mid-1980s.

This is one of the explanations for the fall of the communist regimes. Another is the exhaustion of Marxist-Leninist ideology among the ruling elite, such that, by 1989, most were quite ready to pass the baton to an opposition willing to take power. Some envisioned a combination of market reform and authoritarianism; in Poland, this was known as the "South Korean" faction. But in every country in Eastern Europe there were those who recognized that, thanks both to economic failure and the growing influence (and waning commitment to colonial subsidies) of Mikhail Gorbachev, it made little sense to maintain political power at all costs.

This brings us to Gorbachev himself. That communism fell in 1989–91, and not ten years earlier or later, must be traced to specific turning points and not to structural failures. Gorbachev's accession to power in March 1985 is one such moment; his introduction first of economic reforms (*perestroika*), then civil liberties (*glasnost'*), then democratization, and finally openness to experimentation in the Soviet bloc, undoubtedly helped to encourage reformers in the communist parties to push for even greater openness at home. It is hard to imagine communist parties sitting down to round table negotiations with opposition groups, or agreeing to more-or-less democratic elections, without Gorbachev's implicit permission; the opposition, too, saw hope that the Brezhnev doctrine of intervention to rescue socialism (as in the invasions of Czechoslovakia in 1968 and Afghanistan in 1979) was no longer in effect. For two basic reasons, though, we must be guarded in how much credit we give Gorbachev. First, the course of the revolutions rather quickly escaped from any predictable schema. Gorbachev deserves praise more for *reacting* to revolutionary events in a rational and creative way, rather than for instigating them himself. Second, the opposition in most countries (with the exception mainly of East Germany, which in any case lies outside our focus) had understandable reservations about Gorbachev. He was not the first reformer to inhabit the Kremlin, after all; good intentions were not enough, and his subsequent attacks on independence movements in the Baltics proved this. At any rate, Gorbachev did not articulate his intentions toward Eastern Europe until events there had already advanced very far; not until his address to the European Parliament in July 1989 did Gorbachev clearly state that "respect for each people's sovereign right to choose a social system as it sees fit represents a most important precondition for a normal European process."[3]

Finally, one must credit the growth of opposition in the last two decades of communism. An initial wave of opposition, from 1968 to 1977, consisted largely of intellectuals who sought for a way out of the ideological limitations of the previous era. Rejecting the confines of the Marxism many of them had grown up with, they opened paths to national or religious traditions, and developed programs of "organic work" or "positivism." Czechoslovakia's Charter 77, Poland's Workers' Defense Committee, or Hungary's Committee to Help the Poor sought to bring politics down to earth, to reach out to individual experiences of the communist regime. They laid the foundation for subsequent movements against communism, simply by showing that the limits of what was possible were more breachable than was believed.

Poland's Solidarity – a huge trade union/social movement forged in strikes in August 1980 – was a product of this intellectual fervor, but also of a long tradition of social protest in that country. After wresting trade union autonomy from communist negotiators, Solidarity flourished for sixteen months, creating a deep network of semi-legal publishing houses, self-help committees, political discussion groups, and above all workplace self-governance before General Wojciech Jaruzelski declared martial law in December 1981. Yet unlike previous moments of opposition, such as the Prague Spring of 1968 or the Hungarian Uprising of 1956, Solidarity did not disappear in the face of repression. It survived in the underground, and spawned a whole new generation of grassroots protest movements in every nook and cranny of Polish society. Poles came to realize both that the regime was more toothless than it seemed, and that change – perhaps only at the local level at first – was achievable if one risked standing up to it.[4] In 1988, workers (helped by students of the Freedom and Peace Movement) in several Polish cities went on strike, and this time the regime saw no way out but to agree to negotiations over the very future of the country.

Solidarity, and the hydra that Polish opposition became after the union was outlawed, proved enormously influential across the region. In Czechoslovakia, Hungary, the Soviet Union, and Yugoslavia (as well as East Germany), oppositionists studied Polish tactics, even learning Polish or journeying there to gain experience. Poles, in turn, helped anti-regime movements in neighboring countries. By 1989, networks of opposition stretched across borders from Estonia to Yugoslavia. When 1989 was over, it seemed to many observers that it had been a year of miracles; journalists invoked phrases such as "people power" to describe the sudden outburst that had brought communism down like a house of cards. But communism's fall had not been sudden at all, even though no one had seen it coming (or at least not so soon). Years of doubt, dissatisfaction, discussion, organization, demonstration, and negotiation had tunneled away at the regimes from all angles until not much was left to defend.

The image of dominoes falling suddenly does have some relevance, though. While some countries were more than ripe for revolutionary change, others – such as Romania, or the Serb republic in Yugoslavia – were only just beginning to explore opposition. Still others, like Albania, or the Bosnian and Macedonian republics in Yugoslavia, had not started on that road at all. All would be swept along rather faster toward the end of communism than seemed feasible. Looking back at the fall of communism, in fact, one can hazard a general rule, one likely to be applicable beyond Eastern Europe, too: for peaceful revolutionary change from an authoritarian regime to last, and to produce a transition toward stable democracy, one needs at least a generation of intellectual dissent and a half-decade or more of public, above-ground, varied opposition first.

Several common experiences marked the year 1989 in Eastern Europe, laying the foundations for the post-communist era. First, negotiations played a major role in the revolutions. This may seem a paradox – a negotiated revolution – but after forty-five years of repression of opposition, simulated popular support, and empty democratic forms, the round table discussions of 1989 were indeed revolutionary: the communists, after all, had never before acknowledged an independent partner in society.[5] The trend began in Poland, in February: representatives of the still-illegal Solidarity trade union sat down with communist leaders to find a way out of the political and economic stalemate. The result, after two months of negotiation, opened the path to power for Solidarity: a free press, a re-legalized Solidarity, and semi-free elections to Parliament, in which a newly-created Senate was open to all comers, while seats in the lower house were carefully pre-apportioned to the various sides.

It is remarkable to think that as late as April–May 1989 it did not seem as if change would be swift even in Poland. The communists, with their experience, propaganda skill, and control of the levers of local power, would surely do well in the elections. Even Solidarity activists hoped to win 30–60 seats (of 100) in the Senate. The trick was going to be how to stay out of government, building a strong opposition in order to win an election scheduled for 1993. Yet on June 4 – the same day as the Tiananmen Square massacre in China, and thus a day of divergent paths in the communist world – Poles

voted overwhelmingly for Solidarity candidates, virtually sweeping
the Senate and making the communists seem like also-rans in
a Parliament they nominally controlled. Even more surprisingly,
the communist leadership accepted the election results (though
some Solidarity legislators wondered, even as they took their seats
in Parliament in July, whether this was all a ruse, and they were
about to be rounded up and imprisoned). In August, Solidarity leader
Lech Wałęsa engineered a coup, convincing communist-allied "puppet" parties to jump ship and support a Solidarity government, led
by Tadeusz Mazowiecki – and again both General Jaruzelski and
Mikhail Gorbachev accepted this turn of events. From this point
on, the sense of momentum would begin to build until, by late
November, a feeling of inevitability took hold. The impossible had
become obvious; ironically, this very fact would later make it seem
as if 1989 was nothing so special.

Just two months after the Polish round table, the Hungarian Socialist Workers' Party attempted to follow suit, proposing a
national round table. Like their Polish counterparts, Hungarian
communists surely hoped to manage the course of events; the opposition, which had already convoked its own separate round table
discussions, proved more intransigent and confrontational than
in Poland. While the two sides did agree on free elections for the
following spring, there was much more that divided them; indeed,
the opposition representatives refused even to sign the round table's
final document. While in Poland, Solidarity deputies had reluctantly
allowed for the slimmest of parliamentary majorities to choose General Jaruzelski as president in July, the Hungarian opposition forced
a November referendum on the procedure for choosing a president,
and won. The new president would be chosen by a democratically-
elected Parliament, and the socialist candidate had no chance.

The round table discussions in Prague's "Velvet Revolution"
were immortalized by Timothy Garton Ash, a British journalist
and scholar who watched and participated as the Czech opposition
became a political class. The impetus for change came when police
cracked down on a peaceful (and legal) student demonstration in
honor of those who had resisted Nazi repression, on November 17.
Václav Havel and his colleagues from Charter 77 faced down com-

munist efforts to retain power: first trying to coopt a few opposition figures to a repainted communist government, then trying a reformist coalition, and ultimately acquiescing to a complete changing of the guard. When President Gustáv Husák – the man responsible for the harsh "normalization" of Czechoslovakia after the Soviet invasion of 1968 – resigned on December 10, the way was open for Parliament, purged of some of its most reactionary members but still representative of the old regime, to elect Havel as the new president; elections would follow in the spring of 1990.

By this time, negotiation had become part of the obligatory repertoire of regime change, even though most other countries or republics lacked either a serious opposition partner, or a strong reformist wing in the Communist Party, or both. In Romania in late December, dictator Nicolae Ceauşescu fled (via helicopter from his palace roof) a rally gone wrong, only to be tracked down, subjected with his wife Elena to a summary trial, and executed. In his place there emerged a coalition (itself a kind of negotiation) of communists and oppositionists, the National Salvation Front. After this, the communists in Bulgaria – where Todor Zhivkov had departed peacefully, thanks to an internal party coup earlier that fall – also agreed to a round table.

The prevalence of negotiation is one of the primary reasons that the term "revolution" seems to fit 1989 poorly. Yet the communist system was based upon monologue, in which an elite with the only correct worldview simply conveyed instructions and exhortations to society. "Dialogue" in the past had mostly come in the form of violent outbursts: uprisings bloodily suppressed in the Baltics, Czechoslovakia, Hungary, Poland, or Romania, or reform movements swiftly undermined in Czechoslovakia or Yugoslavia. The very logic of scientific socialism precluded the possibility of competing political viewpoints, much as (if we close our eyes for the moment to the obvious differences) evolutionary biologists reject debate over creationist theories. Dialogue, and political pluralism, were indeed revolutionary concepts in 1989, and they would produce utterly different societies and political systems.

Perhaps inevitably, though, dialogue also excluded many viewpoints. The main partners in discussions with the disintegrating communist regimes would be intellectual elites, mostly espousing some version of liberal nationalism: parliamentary elections, economic reform, restoration of national symbols. For this reason, also, 1989 does not seem revolutionary. The year – and the previous few years, too – had been full of raucous, even joyous demonstrations. East European cities from Tallinn to Sofia had become theaters for the diverse unleashed ambitions of their citizens. Some hoped to live as well as their Western neighbors, and that was for the moment impossible. Others wanted to see all the communists disappear, and that was impractical. But others hoped for an end to old-fashioned elite politics, in favor of a "human" politics, kinder to the earth and its inhabitants, and open to all; a politics that would not simply follow the obvious and easy paths, but take advantage of this great upheaval to create something genuinely new.

That did not happen – although, as I will argue in Chapter 5, the traces of this moral position can be seen in the way Eastern European governments and intellectual elites have tried to act in the world. Every revolution leaves in its wake a sense of missed opportunities, but those missed opportunities deserve a reckoning. The social movements of 1989 did not remake the world's agenda as they might have hoped, but, in a way, they were just as successful. They promoted the freedom to do what one wants, without the strictures of an ideological line and a hidebound bureaucracy. But such freedom, as expressed after 1989, could also mean the freedom to ignore politics altogether, or to pursue a business career, or to espouse a new set of beliefs. The collective euphoria of the fall of communism, or of newly-claimed independence, would fade, and the legacy of that moment would prove to be more complex than at first imagined.

Another common theme was that of national liberation. In a way, this was ironic: the communist regimes had all promoted nationalism. Some had painted themselves as heirs to a great tradition of strong national leaders stretching back a millennium. Others, like Josip Tito of Yugoslavia, had allowed for the development of regional nationalisms, partly to show that communism offered backward peoples the means to realize their cultural aspirations (such as literacy) most fully. Nevertheless, reclamation of national tradition became a central theme. Slovenes protested the exclusive use of Serbo-Croatian in trials of oppositionists; Hungarians reburied their leader in the 1956 uprising, Imre Nagy, as a national hero; Latvians sang folk songs to express their independence from Moscow. Wherever the communist regime had decorated the national flag with symbols of ideology and progress, as in Hungary, Romania, Bulgaria, and the Baltics (as well as East Germany), demonstrators cut these emblems out. Poles, in turn, hoped to add something back, recrowning the heraldic eagle.[6]

Perhaps all this was possible because in 1989 East Europeans quickly came to interpret the communist era as something alien to them. It seemed a hiatus from real history, and thus one should celebrate its end by recapturing that which had been lost fifty years earlier. Of course, it was not a hiatus at all: communist rule changed Eastern Europe and its citizens, most of whom, after all, had never known anything else. But to make sense of the (mostly) peaceful and easy departure of a system in which they had all lived, worked, and grumbled, it was easiest to relabel it as an aberration, not something familiar, and even organic. The past – both pre-communist and communist – would become a central problem and preoccupation in the post-communist era.

There was also the future, of course. *"Europa hned!"* (Europe Now!) was the slogan on buttons and posters everywhere in Prague in February 1990. While there have been many detours, East Europeans have been traveling a road that, they believe, has been taking them to Europe ever since 1989. But what is that Europe that East Europeans saw ahead of them? Most of all, it was free of borders, walls, and ceilings, in which one could travel, have access to goods or ideas formerly inaccessible; and where one could see, or believe, what one wished. In that Europe, one could finally be Czech, or Slovene, or Estonian.

The above formulations will sound, to some readers, like the beginning of a fairy tale. It is quite tempting, in fact, to focus on the ways in which most people's lives have been made easier, richer, freer since 1989. But it is the nature of revolutions that, as the "normal," or at least long-standing, rules are abrogated, people are free to impart to revolutionary change their own meanings. Thus, for some the revolutions meant purity: one could cleanse the nation of those who are different, or cleanse one's past of inconvenient facts, or assert one true moral path as a marker of citizenship. For others, it meant the freedom to leave: a prospect which provoked fear of brain-drains at home, and of floods of semi-skilled labor (such as the ubiquitous Polish plumber, about whom more later) abroad. Most strikingly, Eastern Europeans have asserted an idea of nationhood which sometimes has seemed at odds with the spirit of unification elsewhere in Europe – and with the individualism toward which they also strove.

Commenting on the conflict between collectivity and individuality in Eastern Europe, Slavenka Drakulić notes that "we" was the language of the communist leaders as they exhorted the people to fulfill various plans, and also the language of the homogenized, exclusive nation, while "I" was suspect, as the language both of individual dissent, and of the private pursuit of one's desires and dreams:

> Thus the terrible hypocrisy with which we learned to live in order to survive is having its backlash now: it is very difficult to connect the private and public "I"; to start believing that an individual opinion, initiative or vote really could make a difference. There is still too big a danger that the citizen will withdraw into an anonymous, safe "us" ... "We" means fear, resignation, submissiveness, a warm crowd and somebody else deciding your destiny. "I" means giving individuality and democracy a chance ... [But] a common denominator is still discernible, and still connects us all, often against our will. It is not only our communist past, but also the way we would like to escape from it, the direction in which we want to go. It's our longing for Europe, and all that it stands for. Or, rather, what we imagine Europe stands for.[7]

Today, when a generation of adults who no longer remember the communist era has entered the workforce and the voting booths, and when the entire region is either a part of Europe (in the sense of the EU) or at least negotiating a relationship with it, conflicts within Eastern Europe have less and less to do with post-communism. Yet Drakulić's fears and longings, recorded in 1996, have faded only slightly. Eastern Europe, whatever its boundaries, is a place where the shock of the new still resonates, in the tension between the global and the local, the ideal and the real, the past and the present, and between the "I" and the "we." This book is the story of how the people of the region may have at last found an adjective to replace "Eastern," with all its pejorative connotations: if this is "the New Europe," how did it become so?

1 | Different paths on an open road: economic and social change

On a gray July evening in 1993, there were hundreds of people on the train station platform in the small town of Šestokai, in southern Lithuania, waiting for the train to Poland. The prospective passengers – I was the only one with a reserved seat – were dwarfed by mountains of cargo, for this was the only train connecting the two countries, and thus the best way to transport goods from the Baltics and northern Russia to the bazaars of eastern Poland. My reservation did me little good in the frenzied rush that ensued when the little train finally pulled in. Only with the help of the conductor could I even find a space to stand in the corridor. My assigned compartment was occupied by two Latvian men and their offering to the Polish consumer: several huge milking machines.

In those milking machines, in a Lithuanian border town, we encounter all the mysteries and ambiguities of post-communist economics. How did these passengers come to have such unlikely baggage? How could they know that just such an esoteric item would find a buyer in some Polish town or village? And is this an example of the wonderful ingenuity of modern economic relations, or an illustration of the utter breakdown of law and order, a grotesque parody of globalization enacted by those left on the margins of change? Much depends on perspective – and Western perspectives, since 1989, have been strongly colored by political assumptions. That train was either full of the marginalized and dispossessed, or of wily entrepreneurs building a free market economy suitcase by suitcase. Perhaps we were all right, as we watched Eastern Europe embark on an uncertain journey across once-closed borders.

Those trains filled to bursting are now largely gone, though every bus west from Belarus and Ukraine is destined for the same bazaars, while the milking machines (if there are any left, after all the collective farms have been stripped) now come by truck, shipped by respectable firms. That ingenuity, though, deserves much of the credit for the region's success so far, as well as the blame for some of its suffering. This chapter will explore the most rapid and surprising of all the post-revolutionary transformations: how East European economies and societies evolved into serious competitors with their Western neighbors – into, of all things, "normal" places.

A time for experiments?

In the late communist period, the countries of Eastern Europe were more different socio-economically than they were similar. A few – Albania, Bulgaria, Romania – maintained strict control by plan and police. The Baltic republics of the Soviet Union had emerged under Gorbachev's rule to experiment with cooperatives and nascent social movements. Hungary, Poland, and Yugoslavia had long been at the forefront of efforts to combine private or cooperative economies with central planning; in all three (and to a lesser extent in Czechoslovakia), legal and illegal social activism, especially in the cities, undermined the stereotypes of rigidity and fear. Despite the very real restrictions that communism imposed, Eastern Europe had already accumulated some of the social and economic experience necessary for life outside the cage.

Ultimately, all the countries under consideration here have followed paths toward broadly similar outcomes. Did they have to? Today, the emergence of free market economies, based upon private enterprise, tax incentives, low rates of unionization, and the rest, appears to be inevitable. At the time of communism's collapse, though, some hoped that a "third way" between communism and capitalism could now be found. The best of the socialist system, such as the minimalization of individual economic risk, or collective/cooperative forms, could be combined with the innovation and dynamism of market economies. That such ideas came to nothing – such that throughout the region today, only marginal parties use "third way" language – tells us little about free market inevitability. After all, the conditions in 1989 were such that most people accepted the need for radical change. "Market socialism" was not a promise, but a familiar communist phrase – albeit one from a heretical tradition. Meanwhile, a crisis in West European social democracy meant that international support for experimentation was at an ebb. In another context, the quest for a third way could have been a progressive move, and been eagerly pursued. In 1989, especially since those who talked about it were often from the reformist wing of the old communist parties, it sounded cautious, even fearful.

In 1989–90, the economies of Eastern Europe appeared to collapse with ferocious speed. Industrial production and standards of living plunged, while unemployment and prices rose. Thus, for example, all of the economies of the region saw a decline in GDP in 1990–91, in many cases by over 20 or even 30 per cent. Unemployment went from zero to over 10 per cent in the same period, while inflation hit double or triple digits. This is a bleak picture, but what really happened? It is hard to tell for a number of reasons. First, regime statistics before 1989 cannot be relied upon as benchmarks for what happened later; they tended, for example, to exaggerate economic productivity and underestimate costs; prices in particular made little sense.[1] Second, it is difficult in any case to capture rapid change in annual statistics. And third, as the Latvian milking machine peddlers remind us, so much economic activity remained beyond the reach of any measurement. Millions of East Europeans, moreover, had cash reserves which they had not entrusted to communist banks – the $20 in a Christmas card from an aunt in Chicago, the under-the-table cash earned in a summer picking strawberries in Sweden, the wages of a *Gastarbeiter* husband or son employed in a BMW factory in Munich. This softened the blow, though the hardships of inflation and unemployment would touch everyone. At any rate, the communist economies had been falling apart for at least a decade; the economic and social impact of political change, then, stemmed as much from perception as it did, initially, from actual collapse.

The scope and depth of the revolution also handicapped economic change. Had any one country sought to transform its economy, the results might have been very different; instead, the entire Council for Mutual Economic Assistance (CMEA – the economic organization of communist states, also known as COMECON) faced the same challenges; as a result, export markets for many products disappeared overnight. The collapse of the Soviet Union hit Eastern Europe particularly hard: gone was a guaranteed trade partner, replaced by fifteen fledgling states. Later, war in the Balkans would similarly create trade wars where borders had once been invisible.

Finally, East European leaders had to reckon with social unrest. The nature of that unrest distinguishes post-communist change from previous revolutions. East Europeans are literate, largely urban, and were organized – both in official and independent unions, youth groups, etc. They had struck, marched, rallied, and joined illegal organizations in protest against communist policies. Even before any market reforms had been enacted, workers had shown the regimes (and themselves) what they were capable of. For example, a wave of strikes accompanied Poland's round table discussions of February–April 1989. The Velvet Revolution in Czechoslovakia featured a brief nationwide general strike – the first in that country in twenty years. Millions of others, of course, had participated in non-economic demonstrations in nearly every country in the region in 1989. Who really understood social aspirations, and how people would react to hardship? Reformers throughout the region would have to take this into account.

Unfortunately, 1989 was not the most propitious moment for change. First, the West was experiencing a small recession. A slowdown in the American, Japanese, and Western European economies meant that less attention (and material help) would be paid to emerging economies. Second, the Iraqi invasion of Kuwait in 1990, and the ensuing embargo placed on Iraq by Western allies, led to a drastic reduction in oil deliveries to Eastern European countries; these deliveries had in part been in lieu of debt payments from Iraq. Some countries saw a significant decline in crude oil supplies; all found oil more expensive on the world market just as they were trying to adapt to that market. In addition, most Eastern European countries were heavily in debt to Western banks and governments; Poland owed about $40 billion; Hungary had the highest per capita debt (over $2,500), and owed $20 billion total, while Bulgaria owed nearly $10 billion.[2] Romania, in turn, had paid off its foreign debt under Ceauşescu, but at the cost of utter impoverishment. While

domestic trends are the focus here, the international dimension
(to be discussed in Chapter 5) turned out to be more an obstacle
to change than a bonus.

Still, given the euphoria with which the West – and especially the
United States – greeted communism's demise, many within Eastern
Europe and beyond assumed that a "new Marshall Plan" would be
forthcoming to reward the nations that had ended the Cold War. After
all, the cost of change had turned out to be so much lower, without
war, than anyone could have expected. The amount of aid given may
seem quite large, in the order of $53 billion in official aid from all
sources in the years 1990–98.[3] Yet one estimate pegs grant aid from
the West in the 1990s, in relation to its GNP, as just one-fiftieth of
what the United States had committed to Europe in the 1940s and
1950s.[4] Most aid was in the form of loans or technical assistance, not
grants. There would not be a second Marshall Plan.

There was logic as well as stinginess (or distraction) in Western
policy. Lacking any inkling of the Yugoslav wars just a few years
ahead, the West did not see the same kind of urgency as had been
the case in 1947. Then, fears of a communist takeover of France and
Italy, and of a slide into chaos in Germany, had jolted the US out of
probable isolationism. Forty-three years later, with the Soviet Union
on the wane and no discernible alternative to free market models,
the West could take its time. It could offer instead what Janine
Wedel derisively calls a "Marshall Plan of Advice," in which consultants, credits, and loans replaced straightforward capital assistance.[5]
Furthermore, while the Marshall Plan aid had gone largely to countries that had been either close allies or formidable enemies during
the war (Britain, France, Germany, Italy), the targets in the 1990s
could be assumed to have much less expertise; the main problem,
to Western leaders, was that they had mismanaged economies for
forty-five years – not to mention the fact that some, at least, had
put a lot of energy into economic espionage. Better, then, to keep
tight control over money dispersed. Thus, while Eastern Europe was
not left to its own devices, it would have to bring about economic
transformation on its own.

Hungary and Poland set the pace, in different ways. Poland's
last communist prime minister, Mieczysław Rakowski, began free-

ing prices from state control and eliminating subsidies just weeks before handing over power, in August 1989; ration cards for meat and gasoline, symbolic of communist mismanagement, also finally disappeared. The result – in the absence of any macro-economic policy – was chaos: by early fall, hyperinflation raged and retail trade took to the streets. Every street corner was crowded with farmers selling (presumably) fresh meat and vegetables from the back of small trucks, next to tables piled with new clothing, kitchenware, and books. Perhaps the apparent anarchy made the idea of a "Big Bang" approach to economic reform more appealing. Leszek Balcerowicz, Finance Minister in 1989–91 and 1997–2000 (and later Director of the National Bank), has become most associated with this approach. Just after Christmas 1989, Parliament passed a package of laws designed to hasten the process of marketization. Price liberalization and currency devaluation accompanied strict wage controls (through a tax on excessive wage increases). This was "shock therapy"; its leading international proponent, Harvard economist Jeffrey Sachs, has pointed to Poland's strong economic record as vindication of the approach. The great costs of this shock will be discussed later, meanwhile, one must consider other causes for that success.

Hungary provides an interesting contrast. There, "market social-ism" had been the watchword since the 1970s; prices and wages were not as regulated as they were elsewhere in the region. Still, government subsidies were large, and their phasing out in early 1990 led to unrest, including demonstrations organized by unions and by the center-right Hungarian Democratic Forum. Hungarian leaders, preoccupied with elections and certain of their country's economic superiority, were slower to embark upon economic reform. The belief that Hungary did not need wholesale reform was encour-aging to Hungary's neighbors, but caused problems for Hungary in the long term.

Similar divergence can be seen in approaches to the privatization of state assets. Since state control of industry and land had been one of the hallmarks of communist regimes, there was no doubt at all in the early 1990s that privatization was an essential step. This may not be true, and the programs enacted resulted in a rapid rise in unemployment. Yet it is worth pointing out that privatization of industry was both vastly larger than that undertaken by, for example, Margaret Thatcher in the UK in the 1980s – thousands of firms, rather than dozens – yet also more limited: most countries today do not have privatized infrastructure (transport, oil refineries, post and telecommunications, etc.). Countries as diverse as Slovenia (now by far the wealthiest in the region), Bulgaria (soon to be the poorest in the European Union), and Hungary have chosen to privatize slowly and selectively, despite external advice.[6]

If the task was clear, then, the method was not. The privatization of retail and service (shops, restaurants, etc.) was everywhere uncontroversial, and proceeded quickly. Large manufacturers were another story. Who would buy such dinosaurs, which had operated in accordance with central planning dictates, indifferent to buyers' expectations? One obvious answer was the employees themselves – especially since they were already the owners, according to communist propaganda. Where there were strong unions, employees often demonstrated in support of this approach, or even struck to prevent privatization by other means. Usually, though, employees were offered 10–20 percent of shares in their company, at reduced rates or free. Similarly, there was strong sentiment in favor of mass privatization – that is, distribution of state assets to citizens. Who had made the revolution, after all? Thus emerged the popular idea of citizen vouchers – adopted in Czechoslovakia in 1991, followed by others (particularly Bulgaria, Lithuania, and Poland) in the mid-1990s. Citizens were either allotted vouchers free of charge to be invested in shares of the firm of their choice (or even, in some cases, to buy housing), or were permitted to buy investment vouchers at low cost up to a certain limit and then exchange them for shares in a firm.

The perils and advantages of such a system can be seen in the Czechoslovak case, engineered by the then-Finance Minister Václav Klaus. Each adult citizen could (after paying an administrative fee) acquire a voucher booklet to invest in shares. Most, however, subsequently allocated their shares to investment funds, such as Harvard Capital and Consulting, created by twenty-eight-year-old Viktor Kožený (who had failed to complete his studies at Harvard, but took the name anyway). Kožený (and others like him) ended up a wealthy émigré; few citizens saw the fantastic returns on investment that he promised. Meanwhile, the now-privatized companies derived their capital from state-owned banks. Thus, the Czechoslovak system had succeeded only in transferring ownership from the state back to the state, in the process enriching a few investors. On the other hand, this system did create a kind of "shareholder culture," and moved assets quickly out of the hands of communist managers and the government ministries.

While it is not obvious that investment funds and banks are any more beneficial to the economy and society, as owners, than are the communist *nomenklatura*, resentment of the latter has been a source of a large part of anti-government anger ever since. Throughout the region (but much less so in countries that implemented programs like that in Czechoslovakia), many feel that the communists engineered a takeover of the economy in exchange for relinquishing control of the state – and did so with the connivance of their successors. With their knowledge of the firms they controlled, managers and government officials created complex holding companies to which they sold off assets, or used insider knowledge to acquire majority stakes during privatization.

Given the dearth of capital, and the scarcity of independent managerial ability, there were perhaps no ideal paths to privatization. Vouchers created an illusion of democracy; "nomenklaturization," while easiest, stoked resentment and conspiracy theories. Restitution to former owners could be only a partial solution, and an expensive one at that. That left foreign investment. If Western governments would not be providing Marshall Plan-level aid, could foreign companies be enticed to invest? The problem was not only the decrepitude or decreased value of state-owned firms. An even greater problem was cultural: East Europeans had rightly recognized that their workplaces were not theirs, and most traced ownership back to Moscow, which directed trade within the bloc, even if it did not actually control the assets. Foreign investment implied outside control from another direction. Restrictions on foreign ownership of property, for example, has been politically popular. Yet, while in the early 1990s, citizens across the region expressed fears about foreign investment, and sometimes staged protests (occupying factories, for example), the attitudes were quite different when it came to accession to the European Union. The rhetoric was the same but, this time, East Europeans seemed not to mind.

Soon enough, foreign direct investment rushed in. Through 1994, about $20 billion had been invested in the region. Fully $8.5 billion of this went to Hungary, the country with the most Western exposure (other than Yugoslavia) before 1989, with another $7.4 billion to the Czech Republic and Poland combined. Relative to the size of the economies of investor and target countries, this was a tiny amount; foreign investment, too, has not been the panacea that some once hoped. Robin Okey compares the foreign dependency of industry and finance to that of the 1930s, when Hitler had Eastern Europe in an economic vise well before the war began.[7] One could add that, just as sixty years earlier, Eastern Europe found it had little choice in partners.

The examples thus far have come from the first wave of development. Czechoslovakia, Hungary, and Poland were at the core of economic change in the 1990s, as they had been in the pre-communist period, too. Beyond them were a group of very small and thus quite flexible countries, the Baltic states and Slovenia, able to modernize rapidly after the Soviet Union and Yugoslavia broke apart. Lithuania used vouchers and some auctioning to foreign firms to privatize most state property by 1994. Estonia has used tax incentives to gain foreign investment, benefiting from the intense interest of its Scandinavian neighbors.

The Balkans – if we put aside for the moment the enormous disruption and destruction of the Yugoslav wars – have had much farther to go simply to reach a stage in which any sustained economic development could even be possible. Until recently, macro-economic reform has been more futile than not. One could find no better example than the fate of Ante Marković, Prime Minister of Yugoslavia from March 1989 until December 1991. Like Rakowski in Poland, Marković began by liberalizing prices, which similarly accelerated inflation into the "hyper" zone by the end of the year. While speaking of a Gorbachevian "new socialism," he also instituted, in January 1990, monetary reforms that stifled inflation by that summer; Yugoslavia seemed to have turned the corner toward economic viability.

Political pressures, however, soon derailed these reforms. Whereas in the northern tier and in the smallest countries, leaders like Balcero-wicz could count upon popular and political commitment to change, the mixture of national populism and unreconstructed communism in Yugoslavia and elsewhere in the Balkans gave a different result. Several republics, and especially Serbia, raided the National Bank to pay pensions and bonuses, and fomented opposition to Marković's austerity measures. In 1991, with news of ethnic tensions spreading, Yugoslavia's $4 billion tourist industry disappeared; reforms (and, soon, the country) were history.

While some of the causes were different, the commitment to economic reform was similarly weak in Romania. True, the severe hardship of the late Ceauşescu period left little stamina for belt-tightening or shock therapy. Yet the National Salvation Front, hoping to secure long-term political power in upcoming elections, raised wages, maintained price controls, and avoided revaluing the currency. By 1991, political differences made any decisive reforms impossible. Limited privatization of industry did not begin until 1993, and was undercut by continued reluctance to risk losing the support of state-employed workers. Through the end of the 1990s, Romania faced bouts of hyperinflation, slow growth, and rising debt. Poverty – already painfully evident to the casual visitor in the 1980s – has lingered longer than to the north.

Looking back at the early period of reform, it is hard to avoid a didactic tone. Were the shock therapists right in promoting drastic economic reforms? Knowledgeable East Europeans studied how Sachs's advice had stabilized the Bolivian economy earlier in the 1980s, while condemning most of the urban population to poverty, and shuddered. But Eastern Europe was not Bolivia, and Sachs was not the Headless Horseman, auguring doom wherever he appeared. Indeed, it is too easy to exaggerate the power of neoliberalism in Eastern Europe. The fact that Eastern Europe has changed greatly over the last fifteen years, a time during which neoliberal projects advanced elsewhere (in the creation of NAFTA and the WTO, for example), does not mean that neoliberal programs are responsible for reform in Eastern Europe. Anthropologist Wedel laments the dominance of neoliberal advisors in the brigades that came to

Eastern Europe in the early 1990s. But she also notes the Eastern response: the ability to pretend to listen, while pursuing one's own agenda.[8]

Thus, the story of economic change across Eastern Europe is one of dramatic reform, and of winners and losers. It is not, though, a story of neoliberal hegemony. There are very few examples of "shock therapy," or of total privatization, in the region. Everywhere, economic and social change has been tempered or even directed by popular protest, by foot-dragging (and bureaucratic incompetence), but most of all by the demands of political competition. On the other hand, as government spending on, for example, education or healthcare has declined, one can see in this the indirect effect of the neoliberal program: If governments are not actively trying to get out of the social realm (and there is no evidence that this is so), they are finding that the budget strictures imposed by various international obligations are most easily resolved by limiting outlays on social programs for less-powerful constituents.

Broadly, it seems that in places where reforms took place rapidly, and policies favored foreign investment and entrepreneurship (lowered taxes, limiting of social expenditures), the standard of living has risen the strongest. In countries where difficult choices were avoided, poverty stubbornly hangs on. However, the differences are not mainly due to economic policies. In fact, the conclusion one can draw from this survey is that there is no correct path. Whether countries chose the Big Bang, or gradualism; won the foreign-investment lottery (Hungary's per capita FDI was eight times that of Poland) or employed vouchers, or nomenklaturization, or some combination of these, did not greatly affect their success. More important has been the level of social and economic development *before* the fall of communism. Over the long run, economic success has essentially mirrored relative standing in earlier periods, stretching back even to the nineteenth century. The proximity to Western aid, and to legal or gray-market jobs for migrants, has meant that differing economic programs have not greatly affected success in the north. Moreover, it is not enough to point out that many have been left behind by shock therapy in the Baltics or in Poland; that hundreds of thousands have lost jobs in liquidated firms; and that pensioners on fixed incomes have been unable to enjoy the fruits of change. Inequalities in the economy have also increased, as will be discussed below. But if post-communist Eastern Europe is an experiment, it is hard not to notice that the populist approach in the Balkans has not provided the answer to these problems.

Thus proponents of shock therapy and rapid, ruthless privatization should recognize that countries in the northern tier have been successful no matter what approach they took. All now enjoy more-or-less booming economies, declining unemployment, rising standards of living, etc. It is difficult to separate out causes; for example, membership of the European Union may be both a source of prosperity and an effect. But one thing that does unite all the most successful countries is a record of civic activism and a strong urban infrastructure over the communist era and before. What we might call the Habsburg-Baltic countries had assets that other countries did not. Thus, efforts at reform in Serbia, for example, had less likelihood of success; while other countries where reform stalled, such as Slovakia, succeeded anyway. They were able to count on higher levels of popular support, while ethnic or religious divisions proved less harmful.

More shocks to the system

Rapid, basic economic reform proved even more necessary when, in the latter half of the 1990s, East European countries faced what we might call second-wave problems that threatened to cripple economic recovery. Some of these problems – such as environmental dangers or economic and political corruption – had existed all along, but had long been neglected. Others, like economic crime or the need to reform pensions, healthcare, and administration, grew more obvious precisely as economies began to register positive growth. And still others, ranging from the influx of refugees to the emergence of AIDS to natural disasters and the Russian crash of 1998, would have been hard to predict. Here, there is space to discuss only a few of these issues.

The environmental legacy of the communist era included a vastly inefficient supply and use of energy, especially in the industrial sector (the steel mills that employed tens of thousands of workers consumed much more energy than their Western rivals); severely damaged ecosystems, like the so-called "Black Triangle" of Czech/Polish Silesia, where entire forests had been wasted away by acid rain; and a reliance on nuclear energy from plants of Soviet design (online or under construction in Bulgaria, the Czech Republic, Hungary, Lithuania, Romania, Slovakia, and Slovenia). Overall, these pointed to a political culture that regarded environmental effects as epiphenomena – though, ironically, communist patterns of development did leave large areas of wilderness relatively untouched, while chronic shortages of consumer goods encouraged frugality and recycling. In the early post-communist years, leaders placed reconstruction of the economic and political system, not environmental protection, as a priority. The only major achievement of that period was a marked decline in air pollution, as entire industries ceased to exist.

Only as a measure of stability was achieved, and as accession to the EU became imaginable, did either leaders or societies begin to think seriously about environmental protection as a measure of civilization. But even then, economic development still came first. In 1991, the Slovak government refused to cooperate with a Hungarian decision to end work on a controversial hydroelectric power plant at Gabčíkovo-Nagymaros on the Danube. The Hungarian government was strongly influenced by environmentalists, who had played an important role in communism's fall, and by the project's impact on national culture – it would have flooded or threatened sites associated with Hungarian history. But to the Slovaks, Gabčíkovo (the Slovak part of the project) meant energy independence from the Czechs as well as from the Hungarians (who had once ruled Slovakia). Both countries were trapped between the need for electricity and national pride on the one hand, and international norms on the other. In 1998, after the International Court of Justice required the two countries to reach an agreement on energy production, Hungary unexpectedly (and in the face of massive protests) announced it would restart work on its part of the project. The governing socialists promptly lost power in the election that summer; every successive government has treated the dam project as tantamount to political suicide.

Nuclear plants throughout the region have posed similar dilemmas. Lithuania's Ignalina plant is a good example: with its outmoded Chernobyl-like design, it is a likely candidate for closure, and European negotiators have made closing it a condition of loans and grants, ultimately linking it to Lithuania's accession to the EU. Yet the plant supplies over four-fifths of Lithuania's power, and allows it to export electricity. Ultimately, in this case as in so many others, the problem is that no amount of outside assistance can possibly compensate for the costs of economic reconstruction: the loss of markets, the degradation of the environment, the need for energy independence. It is estimated that compliance with EU directives relating to the environment will cost as much as 110 billion euros – a cost to be borne mainly by the new members.[9]

An analogy can be drawn with the need to maintain social welfare. For many politicians in the first post-communist governments, some communist social welfare policies – extended maternity leave, full employment, liberal disability laws – seemed wasteful almost by definition. The lesson of German unification, in which less-protective West German policies simply superseded those of the annexed German Democratic Republic, was that economic success and access to "Europe" could be achieved only without this baggage. Reformers could console themselves with the argument that these benefits had not been genuine anyway: the healthcare was shoddy, full employment was demeaning, and so on.

Yet the effects were real. A 1996 survey of non-Baltic Eastern Europe estimated that the number of people earning less than $4/day had quintupled since 1989, reaching nearly one-fifth of the population.[10] It is unlikely these numbers have declined; sociologists now speak of a cycle of poverty in the small towns and villages far from national capitals, where jobs – after the closure of local plants and collective farms – are scarce and only the small family garden keeps starvation at arm's length (malnutrition among schoolchildren, for example, is now recognized as a serious problem). In the cities, older high-rise apartments, once the pride of communist modernity, have become vertical slums, spawning distinctive hip-hop cultures that have largely supplanted the skinheads of the last decade, but which are no less an expression of anger and despair. It is now clear that economic transformation by itself will not eliminate poverty, even with high GDP growth rates.

What was hidden in the communist era is now open. Poverty had a different meaning before 1989; while many basic needs (sanitary napkins, telephones, various foodstuffs, for example) were in severe shortage, most people would not have considered themselves poor. Similarly, what is new today is not wealth – after all, the communist elite sometimes flaunted its riches, too – but an affluent upper middle class of entrepreneurs, consultants, bankers, and company vice-presidents. To be poor today in Eastern Europe also means to be isolated, as the dense network of local buses, village libraries, and state-run political organizations has thinned, while the tattered infrastructure – crumbling roads, non-existent phone lines – hampers participation in the internationalizing economy. The question today is whether increased affluence in the cities, and accession to the European Union, will bring greater awareness of and concern about poverty, or simply entrench these social differences.

The biggest losers in Eastern Europe are the refugees. The Bosnian war sent some 2.5 million from their homes; most stayed within Bosnia-Hercegovina, while perhaps a million escaped to Croatia, to Western Europe, and to the United States. The war in Croatia sent several hundred thousand Serbs from their homes, most never to return. Finally, the Kosovo war nearly emptied Kosovo of Albanians; most of them, unlike their predecessors, found immediate, if temporary, shelter at NATO bases, and were able to return home within a year. The 200,000 Serbs and Roma displaced during or after that war were not as fortunate. The common experience of all these refugees is to feel unwelcome on both sides of the border. With some 300,000 Yugoslav refugees still abroad, plus far more nominally returned yet blocked from their homes, the scars of forced displacement will take long to heal.[11] One major effect has been on recipient countries. During the Kosovo war, Albania and Macedonia took in more refugees than any Western country had during the entire decade of Yugoslav warfare. This was a nearly impossible burden for struggling economies.[12]

The gaps in the social safety-net left behind after communism have been partially filled by churches. This role was evident in a few countries (mainly in Poland and Croatia) before 1989; now, both mainstream and newcomer churches play an important role in communities, distributing goods and providing assistance to pensioners, the unemployed, or the disabled. They also anchor neighborhoods and villages, in addition to their role in national culture. Even as churches are inherently exclusive and divisive – the services provided depend upon doctrine, and assistance usually comes with an evangelical price-tag – their activity has undoubtedly helped to lower the pain of socio-economic transformation, for some. For just this reason (beyond spiritual factors), "new" churches, ranging from Baptists to Seventh-Day Adventists to Mormons, have found a foothold in some communities, while familiar ones – the Roman Catholic Church in the Czech Republic or Hungary, or Islam in Bosnia-Hercegovina – have revived where they were somewhat dormant in the communist era.

A good measure of the strength of a society is its ability to withstand unexpected strains. One spectacular failure was that in Albania in 1997. In the absence of a reliable banking system, many Albanians were attracted to various pyramid schemes which promised fantastic returns on investment. Given the almost unlimited possibilities for arms smuggling and money-laundering in the Balkans during the Yugoslav Wars, these schemes delivered impressive returns on hundreds of millions of dollars in the years 1994–95. To Albanians who sold their houses to invest, it seemed as if capitalism would give them something for almost nothing. When the schemes finally, inevitably, collapsed in the winter of 1996–97, thousands of cheated investors took to the streets, demanding that the government (which had turned a blind eye for years) refund their lost savings. During the uprising in the south, rioters looted police armories; several thousand died and tens of thousands more fled the country by boat across the Adriatic to Italy, as they had in 1991. A collapse of the government followed. There had been similar pyramid schemes in other countries – Romania in 1994, for example, or Poland in 1989 – but the level of faith, or desperation, in Albania was something different.

In comparison, when disaster struck the Czech Republic and Poland in 1997, the results were rather subdued. Torrential rains in early June of that year led to record flooding on both sides of the mountains of Lower Silesia. The floods caused over 100 deaths and billions of dollars in damage. In neither country did voters punish politicians for the ensuing chaos, though in both the floods contributed to an economic slowdown that ended several boom years and hastened the fall of the Klaus government in the Czech Republic. Even just a few years after the economic transformation began, the capacities of societies to absorb challenges varied greatly.

A different kind of economic crisis hit the entire region in August 1998, when Russia defaulted on short-term debts and devalued the ruble. That crash was emblematic of the end of the first phase of post-communist economic growth. Basic privatization had been accomplished, while foreign investments had long since become more important than economic assistance (except in former or future war zones). The easier reconstruction had been either completed or – as in the cases of the Albanian pyramid scheme, or the Czech bank collapse of late 1996 – exposed as faulty.

Now the harder work began. Countries began to pay more attention to their international ratings from Moody's or Standard & Poor's, and sought to attract investment through various tax schemes. Estonia abolished taxes on reinvested corporate profits in 1999; Slovakia instituted a flat income/corporate tax rate in 2004. Assessment of these schemes can be left to economists and investors; from the historian's perspective, one can see a symbolic shift from countries seeking aid as victims of hardship to countries competing with each other, and with their Western neighbors, as sites of investment.

A balance sheet, from the perspective of the East European citizen, is hard to draw up. Overall, the result is a rapid rise in overall standards of living. In the 1980s, average wages amounted to just tens of dollars per month. Now, Slovenia's per capita income stands at 80 per cent of the EU average, and is thus comparable to that of Greece. The Czech Republic, Slovakia, and Hungary are also above half the EU average, with the Baltic states and Poland close behind.[13] Recent studies have also noted that, after rising inequality in the early transition years, the trend may be reversing in the best-off countries at least. Yet large groups of people, especially the Roma, as well as the residents of many rural areas, have not been so fortunate.[14]

Their economic transition resembles the communist-era housing blocks that have been repainted in bright colors while the standard of living inside stagnates.

Movements after revolution

The socio-economic transformation of Eastern Europe is not, however, simply a story of macro-economic policy; nor can it end with a brief discussion of the winners and losers in that transformation. The people of Eastern Europe have been actively involved in the remaking of their homes. Protest of government social and economic policies has been a nearly constant factor, but not the only one. That environmental, welfare, and social issues have been debated at all is thanks to a myriad of social movements that have articulated alternative politics. Finally, in the last half-decade, charitable giving has emerged in the wealthier countries. All these trends suggest that civil society is a strong force in the region. As a new generation of social movements have emerged in Eastern Europe, however, the resultant landscape is rather different from that in the West.

Some countries came into the post-communist era with long traditions of civic activism. For Czechs, Slovaks, Hungarians, Poles, Slovenes, and, to a lesser extent, the Balts, the problem was how to adapt illegal or semi-legal forms of activity to democracy. Workers, students, and peasants needed to decide whether strikes or demonstrations against a truly representative government had the same meaning as strikes under communism. Some believed the new governments deserved a honeymoon period; others felt that one had to continue to articulate demands and aspirations in public ways, and not only at the ballot box. In the rest of the region, the problem was lack of civic involvement of any kind. Unless one counts the largely ceremonial referenda concerning independence, citizens of these countries had done little to undermine communism through collective action. How could civil society now be created or encouraged? Popular activism in the Balkans, meanwhile, consisted primarily of political rallies (sometimes summoned by the regime, sometimes seeking to topple the regime) or nationalist mobilization.

In retrospect, no country was more likely to face massive social unrest than Romania. Given the brevity of mobilization in 1989, the public had little sense of alternative forms of civic engagement; there was no intermediary between society and the government. In January 1990, truckloads of miners from the Jiu Valley came to Bucharest to demonstrate their support of the National Salvation Front, at a time when student activists were publicly questioning whether the revolution had been genuine. The miners won from the Front a series of agreements on wages, pensions, taxes, and working conditions. Thus had workers wrested concessions from communist regimes for decades; the NSF soon found, however, that these promises were impossible to fulfill, as Nicolae Ceauşescu's regime had drained the country dry. Even the promise of a five-day working week had to be postponed. Spring 1990 saw a cascade of protest: miners, dockworkers, railway conductors, autoworkers, bus and subway workers all struck or threatened strikes. With the country's first free elections on the horizon, the NSF agreed to all strikers' demands – though those demands were in reality unsustainable without economic reform. Though a presidential advisor warned of "a great shock as people start realizing that what they demand in living standards will have to be paid for with hardship,"[15] the government managed to avoid that hardship for many years.

For the Front, the payoff was political; economic reform and actual improvement in the standard of living could wait for future governments. In June, the miners came back, this time to attack student demonstrators occupying University Square; as many as twenty-one people died in the clash, with hundreds seriously injured.[16] And the next year, the miners again returned to Bucharest, this time to protest declining economic conditions; they provoked the fall of the government. The common thread here is the intertwining of economics and politics in a way that evokes the paternalism of the communist era. Governments would rise and fall depending upon their perceived ability to satisfy societal economic demands immediately. It was this same perception that allowed Slobodan Milošević to raid the banks and eviscerate the Marković reforms in Yugoslavia, or Albania's Parliament to tolerate pyramid schemes.

Not that northern countries lacked protest. In October 1990, taxi and truck drivers protesting a 66 percent hike in gasoline prices (linked by the government to declining Soviet oil deliveries) paralyzed Hungary for three days, blockading intersections and highways. Polls showed Hungarians in strong support of the strikes, despite the inconvenience. Poland, in turn, saw frequent strikes and street protests in the first post-communist years (and since) – in fact, protest did not seem to decline at all after the fall of communism, and was far higher than among its neighbors. In 1990, striking railroad workers and dairy farmers paralyzed northern Poland; miners protested in November. By 1991, it seemed as if every month brought new strikes, or mass demonstrations in Warsaw. As Grzegorz Ekiert and Jan Kubik write: "Collective protest became entrenched in the political landscape and a routine strategy for advancing various political and economic claims."[17] The result in each country, though, was what Mitchell Orenstein calls "democratic alternation":[18] Instead of crackdown, or abandonment of economic reform, there was compromise, often under a new government. The Hungarian government reduced the price increases, while the Poles moderated shock therapy.

There were two key differences between North and South in this respect: first, northern societies had experienced (and then largely abandoned) unmediated, violent protest during the communist period, and had discovered the limitations of paternalism. Second, these governments had gained power partly through negotiation; many politicians had begun their careers exposing regime secrecy, and thus had at least to pretend to transparency. While Poles lampooned Labor Minister Jacek Kuroń's weekly television addresses, and his campaign to provide soup to the hungry, such tactics helped to defuse anger, too. In post-communist Eastern Europe, economic/political protest has flourished where conspiracy theories were strongest. While many observers at the time felt that any social protest was a bad thing, either because it disrupted the delicate process of transformation or was a harbinger of extremist populism (or both), the value of protest lay in its context.

Worker protest was particularly poignant, as the relationship between identity and politics had changed so much over the last few decades. In Europe, at least, class had lost much of its salience as a mobilizing force; it now competed with individual, issue-oriented identities, with gender, and (increasingly) with nation and ethnicity. The communist regimes had at least pretended that class was a primary (though not solitary) identity; their collapse brought down class as well. The disintegration of trade unions and class-based parties after communism also hampered social protest in the 1990s. Real socialist parties (as opposed to those that were simply repainted regime parties) generally failed to revive, in line with Minister Kuroń's observation that while he would rather be in socialist opposition to a capitalist order, it looked as if he would have to help build the latter first.

State-sponsored trade unions, in turn, lost their raison d'être: not because they were irrelevant in the new age of capitalism (far from it!), but because they had been so strongly identified with the communist regimes. Their main function had not been advocacy of workers' rights and demands, but as mobilizers of labor in the service of regime requirements. They were no more trade unions than the communist parties had been parties. After communism, the old unions devoted much of their effort to retaining their considerable assets (or disposing of them as painlessly as possible), and to finding a unionist, or populist, language that would ring true.

Two great exceptions were Poland's Solidarity and Bulgaria's Podkrepa (Support). Both had formed in opposition to their communist regimes – Solidarity in 1980, Podkrepa in February 1989. Podkrepa had the relative luxury of continuing in opposition to the ruling Socialist Party for much of the 1990s; on the other hand, this left it in the awkward position both of defending workers' interests (for example, by supporting a strike wave in early 1990) and advocating a swifter transition to a market economy. That its leader, Dr. Konstantin Trenchev, openly advocated the restoration of the Bulgarian monarchy did not help. Solidarity's position was more difficult still. The new government in 1989 was strongly identified with Solidarity; in December 1990, its former head, Lech Wałęsa, was elected President of Poland. At the beginning, Solidarity leaders saw themselves as providing a protective cover for the government, but this is not normally what trade unions do. Much of Poland's first post-revolutionary decade was shaped by this search for a post-dissident identity.

At the same time, Solidarity, like Podkrepa, had to contend with reinvented former communist unions. They, like their counterparts elsewhere in the region, had no difficulty in staking out an anti-reform, pro-worker position generally to the left of their erstwhile communist allies; such unions often competed for members by demonstrating their radicalism. An alternative approach was tripartite arrangements, first established in Hungary in 1988 and in Czechoslovakia in 1990, but now common across the region. Regular meetings between the government, the unions, and employer representatives establish objectives on wages, so as to defuse labor conflict. The result, however, has not been real power for labor, as employers have no particular reason to buy into any corporatist arrangement, and governments do not make the agreements binding.[19]

Another reason for the decline of traditional social movements is the effacing of a social class unique to the region: the intelligentsia. In the communist period, and before, the prestige of the intellectual was very high, even among those who were not literate. That prestige drew strength both from national traditions – in a region where national cultures usually developed before modern political states – and from the communist emphasis on propaganda and education. The relatively liberal financing of cultural institutions and periodicals, for example, was evidence of the position of intellectuals in the communist states: what Miklós Haraszti called the "Velvet Prison."[20] Many intellectuals had used their skills and/or influence to advance reformist and oppositional ideas, and – especially but not only in Poland – forged alliances with workers against communists. For better or worse, that role disappeared after communism's fall. State subsidy of culture dropped precipitously; theaters and publishing houses closed their doors. Many intellectuals emigrated; in Bulgaria, which suffered the worst "brain-drain" of the region, it is estimated that nearly two-thirds of younger scientists left between 1990 and 1998.[21] Still more entered business or politics, leaving academia or the art world behind. Now, with the exception of some nationalist groupings, parties can no longer boast the intellectual pedigree they once could. The preoccupation with economic success has surely left behind ideas as well as people.

Left behind by economic change yet symbolic of Western trends;

emblematic of the old system's priorities while advocating social progress: women and women's movements in Eastern Europe have been both victims and victors of the revolution. Communist states empowered women rhetorically and numerically. The regimes advocated women's full access to the workforce, and placed women in public roles (Parliament and the courts in particular) that Western countries could rarely match. Yet that power was illusory; numbers did not add up to influence. In communism, the traditional double burden became triple, as a long "shift" standing in grocery-store queues joined the factory and home shifts. Women's organizations, like trade unions, were not advocacy groups but transmission belts running from government to people, and not the other way around.

In the post-communist era, women were often first to lose their jobs – though some, like accountants, now found that skills stigmatized under communism were suddenly in demand.[22] Women's movements, in turn, were caught in a double trap, seen as both a communist legacy and a harbinger of unwelcome Western influence. Still today, post-communist parties generally account for the largest share of women members of Parliament. Nowhere have feminist movements gained a prominent public voice, though they are active everywhere: in gender studies programs at universities, in magazines and collectives, and in public campaigns for women's issues. They have had particular resonance, though, in the Balkans; their importance there may tell us something about feminism's future in Eastern Europe. The Yugoslav wars exposed women's disempowerment in a radical way, making the world aware that rape could be and was used as a weapon of war. Discussion about violence against women has elsewhere been seen, by post-communist publics, as an intrusion into or recasting of family relations. The mass rapes in Bosnia in 1992–95 grabbed international attention, but have had a profound effect in the former Yugoslavia. Feminism, in this context, did not seem so much radical as it was necessary. Groups like Mothers Against War, which appeared across Yugoslavia in 1991, or B.a.b.e. (Be Active, Be Emancipated – the acronym works in Croatian as well), or the STAR Network of local women's cooperatives, both founded in Zagreb in 1994, are examples of this activism.

The rest of Eastern Europe is today awakening to smaller, more hidden examples of violence against women. Like wartime rape, trafficking in women (and children) is an issue that speaks both to feminism and to nationalism. The trade has targeted rural women, especially from poorer former Soviet countries, but also from the Balkans. The wealthier countries of Eastern Europe are sometimes simply a transit stop on the way to sex rings in Western European countries, but cities like Budapest have a thriving sex industry. In the years before the EU expansion, highways leading into Eastern Europe from the West were lined with women offering their services. Another destination (as has been true throughout history) are the NATO military bases associated with the Bosnian and Kosovo wars.[23] A lesser-known phenomenon is illegal labor: domestic and childcare help among the rising middle class, for example, is often provided by well-educated women from Ukraine. These closer encounters with women's exploitation are helping to domesticate feminism, as it were, transforming it from foreign ideology to native concern.

One problem for feminist movements is the ambiguity of the changes in women's lives since 1989. On the one hand, women have disproportionately lost jobs and been deprived of rights – extended maternity leave, access to abortion – guaranteed by some (but by no means all: Romania was a prominent exception) communist countries. On the other hand, few women regret the end of communism's perquisites (though they may miss the remembered economic security); full employment, after all, meant it was difficult to have the freedom not to work. And if the media today promote images of middle-class domesticity, fueled both by Western market models and by nationalist home-and-hearth doctrines, women's magazines and television also feature new versions of success for women – as entrepreneurs, as politicians, as cultural figures.

The predominant form of non-nationalist social activism in the post-communist era is environmental. Green issues entered most citizens' consciousness in April 1986, when Chernobyl's radioactive cloud seeped across the region. For East Europeans, green politics is not at all abstract, as the threats to health and livelihood can be easily seen and felt. Indeed, ecological concerns resonate well with the rhetoric of dismantled barriers that has had such a powerful pull on the East European imagination. When the walls, curtains, or barbed wire came down in 1989, Eastern Europe became vulnerable to many unexpected influences: in the face of black clouds, AIDS, multi-national companies, GMOs, and refugees, it is easy to see why green politics, and sometimes also human rights and anti-globalist politics, can be nationalist, too. Peasant parties, for example in Croatia, have been vocal in opposition to GMOs. Extremist parties have also gone green, citing environmental hazards as just another threat from the West. Environmental attitudes are traditionally assumed to be related to standard of living. With their experience of communist disdain for the environment – for many East Europeans symbolized by the waste left behind by departing Soviet troops in the early 1990s – citizens of the region show as much environmental consciousness (concern about pollution, understanding about human–environment interactions, etc.) as do their more developed neighbors.[24]

To market

Eastern Europe's societies had several advantages, some of them unexpected, as they began their economic transformation. To recap: As largely urban, educated, trained societies, they have rebounded quickly – and the stronger these attributes were, the stronger was the rebound. Small countries (all but two are smaller than 11 million people) have been particularly able to restructure their economies. Finally, the closer a country is to Western Europe, the better it has fared. Deep (though often latent) resources in church and national traditions, while shutting some out from opportunities, have shaped responses to change in both positive and negative ways. Most important of all, the communist experience has proven to be more of an asset than was expected. Once, it was assumed that communism taught people to be lazy, and to expect to be (more or less) cared for in return for obedience. But the shortages and mismanagement endemic to the old system also bred a resourcefulness that has translated well to the era of the free market.[25]

As the borders opened, the roadside stalls became international bazaars for the "suitcase trade," spilling across public squares in city centers. For the first time in a century, Eastern Europe became a crossroads of commerce. Russians and Ukrainians came west to sell small quantities of caviar, children's clothing, and Soviet memorabilia; East Europeans criss-crossed the region, selling whatever foodstuffs happened to be cheaper or more available in one place than another – not to mention those who found that they could even move the machinery discarded by (or stolen from) collective farms. Both Berlin and Vienna had bazaars nicknamed "Polenmarkt," where one could buy goods or hire workers from the East. Germans and Austrians hungry for bargains crossed their eastern borders by the millions. The highways into Hungary now were crowded with signs advertising affordable dentistry; those into Poland, with small shops offering plaster garden gnomes to the insatiable German taste for kitsch. Romania became one of the leading sources for adoption, selling off children from its overcrowded orphanages to wealthy Western parents until EU-forced legislation virtually shut down this export in 2002. And those who sought greater profits turned to smuggling. Truckloads of cigarettes, vodka, and gasoline streamed across all the borders of the region, with the help of bribed customs officers.

It is estimated that, in 1993, the "hidden economy" peaked at one-third of Hungary's GDP, declining to about one-fifth by 1998. In Romania, the informal or underground share of the economy remained around 40 percent through 2000.[26] Not only individual households, then, but entire economies have been built on the home-grown onions sold on the local market, the Turkish T-shirts sold at the urban bazaar, the folk art sold by the highway, the off-hours plumbing work, the summer jobs bussing tables in London or crushing grapes in France, and the bribes taken as some of these goods and services are arranged. It is worth remembering that most of this activity – as well as, of course, large-scale smuggling – goes untaxed, beggaring the treasuries of developing states.

One result has been a change in attitude toward independent economic activity. In the communist era, such enterprise had negative connotations. If not forbidden, it was at least shameful, compared to honest wage work. This lasted into the early post-communist period, too. Those who crowded buses to peddle cartons of cigarettes or bags of jeans hundreds of miles away were despised – even as people made the bazaar part of their weekly shopping. But trade has largely lost its negative connotations. True, the bazaars have mostly disappeared from urban areas in EU-member countries (except for weekend flea markets), but they have been replaced by weekly shopping trips to the discount store. As the boundaries between legal and illegal have become more sharply defined, the moral questions about trade have subsided.[27]

The nature of formal business has changed, too. In the first post-communist years, business meant restructuring and privatization of established firms, and the arrival of multi-nationals. An American consultant was a common accessory, though foreign consultants – known in Poland as the "Marriott Brigade" for their fancy, fly-by-night tastes – often knew little about local conditions and had less interest in finding out. When I visited Prague's Staropramen Brewery in 1995 with a group of American MBA student-executives, the appearance of a young American advisor, bounding out of his office with snappy asides about the NBA playoffs, evoked a collective sigh of relief; the students had encountered a wearying succession of older managers with communist-era experience and little English. On a similar visit to Warsaw ten years later, it was the Polish managers who impressed the business students most – such as Dr. Irena Eris, the founder of an eponymous cosmetics firm that now employs several hundred, exporting across Europe and to the Americas, who described her firm's strategy and goals in fluent, infectious English.

This dynamism and enthusiasm – exemplified by one young Polish consultant who told my students, "I don't believe in technological problems in the twenty-first century" – capture a shift in focus. While privatization and multi-national investment have brought billions of dollars into East European economies, new firms, and especially small and medium-sized enterprises, account for most of the growth in employment and revenue.[28] No less significant in cultural terms is the decline of the American expatriate. Economic expansion today is largely a native, or at least European, affair.

Nevertheless, a strong current of nostalgia remains. Surveys consistently show a majority of those old enough to remember communism in every country – even well-off Slovenia – expressing some fondness for the good old days. Leaving aside for now attitudes toward the politics of the past (the subject of Chapter 3) these responses tell us a lot about economic and social change, too. For the most part, and especially in the 1960s and 1970s, one's socio-economic position in communist Eastern Europe was secure and certain. While for many – especially in Romania and Albania, but also in urban areas throughout the region – that might mean a standard of living unacceptable to peers in Western societies, millions of others can recall a secure job and access to comforts unimaginable a generation before. In contrast, post-communism is by definition uncertain. The economy now rewards and punishes risk; few jobs are guaranteed.

East European societies, meanwhile, have become more mobile. Perhaps that statement should be modified, for the post-communist era was just another chapter in a restless history stretching back, at least, to the refugees of World War One. As the barbed wire came down, millions left Eastern Europe for the EU, either temporarily or permanently. Most countries did not really notice the loss, but some 40 percent of all working-age Albanians, for example, left for work abroad at some point in the years 1994–98.[29] Yet migration for work in Western Europe is even less of a one-way trip than it used to be. Similarly, movement to a city is not permanent. East European populations have proven more flexible than was expected. In 1990, Western Europe feared a massive influx of economic refugees from the East. By and large, that has not happened – with the exception of movement from East to West Germany, and the refugees from the Bosnian War. By 1993, net migration from the future EU members (plus Bulgaria and Romania) had dropped to zero. As of 1998, there were about 350,000 Poles and 120,000 Romanians in the EU (among recent migrants); the numbers from other countries were vastly smaller.[30] Yet the fears have remained, as we shall see in discussion of the EU expansion, in Chapter 5. Meanwhile, as noted earlier, Eastern Europe is coping with in-migration of its own, from countries further east.

The outlook on Eastern Europe's economy, from the perspective of 2005, is quite positive even in the least successful countries. Economies are growing at a fast pace, while recorded unemployment is falling. This is in large part thanks to the stimulus provided by the accession (or the hope of accession) to the European Union – the freer trade movement of goods, services, and people, along with the regulatory stimulus on quality, have had an obvious effect.

But from a historian's perspective, some caution is in order. If Eastern Europe has not found a third way, it is not at all clear that it has found the right way, either. If one-fifth of the population is below the poverty line, and if that proportion is much higher in some areas, then the economic transformation cannot be said to have been successful. The blame for that failure lies in part with the West, for withholding aid, and for facilitating the conflicts in the Balkans that have left that region practically destitute. In part, the fault is communism's: Poverty and unemployment have not been created by the economic transformation, but by the economic and social policies of the previous decades. And in part, the fault lies with those who would push failure to the margins. For relative prosperity cannot be considered by itself; subsequent chapters will consider the experience of minorities and the potentially corrosive effects of chauvinist nationalism; and the difficulties encountered in coming to term with the crimes (and the mere acquiescences) of the past. Post-communist society is still very much a work in progress, and thus extraordinarily difficult to capture in a historical framework.

Economic and social reform in Eastern Europe has engendered a reconsideration of citizenship, and of the obligations of the state. Attitudes have changed: In 1990 many East Europeans (especially in the more successful north) were prepared to accept the neo-liberal mantra that progress necessitated increased inequality and declining services; since then, they have found their own ways forward. The EU enlargement in 2004, and subsequent suspension of further expansion, meanwhile, have removed significant incentives for reform. Formerly communist parties and populist movements have benefited politically from this retreat. As a whole, however, Eastern Europe is on a different road today from the one it traveled before 1989 – or more accurately, it is riding in a different way. In a debate in November 1988, communist trade union official Alfred Miodowicz assured Polish television viewers that "We are going in the direction" of a modern, efficient economy. His opponent, Lech Wałęsa, riposted: "Yes, you are going – but step-by-step, on foot. And the world is going by car."[31] Maybe Eastern Europe was riding in the back seat, and could not be certain of the route, but it was now on board.

2 | In praise of ethnic cleansing? National struggles

There was once a time – before wrangling over the Euro, EU expansion, and the EU constitution; before antisemitic vandalism in France reached new heights; before the firebombing of refugee hostels in Germany; before Silvio Berlusconi and Jörg Haider – when it seemed that nationalism in Europe was losing its ancient grip. As Western Europe moved into ever-closer cooperation, and as prosperity spread outward from the old European Economic Community's core, divisions based upon cultural–ethnic difference were fading, so it was argued. Only on the geographic margins (in Northern Ireland, the Basque country) or on the exotic fringe (Le Pen's Front National in France, for example) would one find a persistent devotion to a fading source of exclusive identity.

The events of 1989 seemed to confirm that nationalism was a crutch for less-developed societies. All those newly freed from communism expressed their liberation in national terms (even if they also talked about "Europe"), and sometimes seemed more interested in competition than cooperation. A joke then circulating in Yugoslavia captured this difference nicely:

> "How many countries will there be in Europe in the year 2000?"
> "Seven: Europe, Serbia, Croatia, Slovenia, Bosnia, Montenegro, and Macedonia."

It sometimes seemed, in the 1990s, as if that joke was coming true. But in fact, nationalism has been rediscovered – hiding in plain sight – all across the continent. Nor is it clear that it is a negative force, nor a relic of more primitive urges in the human brain. What is more, the most base expression of nationalism in politics, the desire to draw lines to exclude people unlike oneself – that is, ethnic cleansing – has come to seem almost acceptable. The last fifteen years, in short, have posed difficult questions about the relationship between ethnicity on the one hand and democracy, stability, and prosperity on the other.

To the crowds that victorious autumn, 1989 seemed a celebration of liberty's recovery, a return to the halcyon days before 1939. Yet just as nationalism had not withered away in Western Europe, so too nationalism (as opposed to sovereignty, which had suffered) had not been suppressed, or sent into exile, in communist Eastern Europe. Quite the contrary: in most countries, it had flourished. Communism, it is true, had internationalism at its heart: rather than accepting ethnic or religious affinity with their bourgeois masters, workers would recognize brotherhood with proletarians everywhere, and the state would cease to promote national culture and instead fade away. Indeed, the very expansion of Soviet control into Eastern Europe during and after World War Two was a warped expression of this internationalist ideal. Even those countries that broke away from the Soviet bloc – Yugoslavia and Albania – did so not only to reassert national sovereignty, but also to forge new versions of proletarian unity. Yugoslavia was active in the Non-Aligned Movement, linking states independent of either side in the Cold War, while Albania forged an alliance with its distant soulmate, China.

As Stalinist mobilization lost its punch in the 1950s, though, most regimes found recourse to nationalist pride as a source of legitimacy. They sponsored mega-productions of famed historical epics (even, in Hungary, a rock opera on medieval themes); promoted folk culture – like the fictitious "Ride of the Kings" in Milan Kundera's *The Joke* – and encouraged nationalist cults of personality. Romania's Nicolae Ceauşescu was only the most egregious beneficiary of such a cult; Todor Zhivkov in Bulgaria, Josip Tito in Yugoslavia, János Kádár in Hungary, and Poland's Edward Gierek all used national themes – such as personal suffering, or links to the land – to enhance their leadership. Whether or not the wolf had merely donned eagle's clothing, this reframing gained some measure of acquiescence, and support, from society.

Meanwhile, communist regimes in the federal states – the Soviet Union, Yugoslavia, and to a lesser extent Czechoslovakia – promoted ethnic affirmation, celebrating the attributes of all the constituent nations. In the Soviet Union, this meant mostly that Estonian folk dancers, for example, could be found on national television, scheduled between Uzbek and Moldovan troupes. But the federal structure of these states also placed minority nations – Latvians, Macedonians, Slovaks – alongside and equal to the majority, and maintained their capitals and internal borders, too, eventually making it easier for them to break away.

Thus, nationalism today is a legacy of communism. For example, one can argue that the social welfare programs of many conservative parties (see Chapter 4) would be unlikely without the communist idea of the nation. Most of all, communist-era nationalism linked nation to state more powerfully than had ever been the case before. Though nationalist rhetoric in 1989 trumpeted a reawakening, what was at stake was rather a reevaluation of nation. What did it mean to be a Croatian, a Lithuanian, a Hungarian after 1989? Was an emigrant, or a minority, a member of the nation? Could one be a member of the nation yet not a citizen? These are questions that make sense anywhere; the cases of post-communist Eastern Europe simply pose them very directly.

Nationalist extremes

It may seem surprising to assert that state-centered nationalism has weakened since 1989. Yet consider the utter failure of a prime example of "reawakened" nationalism, often heralded in the early 1990s: monarchism. For a few years, deposed kings or their heirs were everywhere: King Michael of Romania, who had abdicated and gone into exile in 1947, tried repeatedly to return to the country, and claimed that he still considered himself the lawful head of state. Tsar Simeon II of Bulgaria, deposed in 1946, similarly showed much interest in returning home, though not necessarily as king; several parties began discussing the revival of the monarchy. Archduke Otto von Habsburg, the eldest son of the last Austro-Hungarian emperor, let it be known that he would be willing to run for president of Hungary. Heirs to the Yugoslav and Albanian thrones also reappeared. What more poetic illustration of Eastern Europe's timelessness than to see the dynasties (some of them not so ancient) restored?

In the end, all the thrones remained empty. Michael attempted

to visit Romania in December 1990; he was detained, accused of attempting to sneak into the country, and unceremoniously expelled. A
year and a half later, he returned in triumph, his motorcade cheered
by hundreds of thousands. Yet while some chanted slogans like "The
Monarchy Will Save Romania!," most were probably simply curious
to see what a king looked like.[1] When he returned to the country
again, in early 1997, only a few hundred greeted him at the airport.
A 1998 poll (commissioned by the royal family) found only about 10
per cent of Romanians interested in giving monarchy a try; Michael's
nephew, Prince Paul Hohenzollern, garnered even less support when
he attempted to run for president in 2000.

Bulgaria came close to holding a referendum on the monarchy,
in 1991. Because of his relative youth and his good command of
Bulgarian, Simeon II's popularity rose quickly, to 42 per cent in a
December 1990 poll.[2] Like Michael of Romania, Simeon II made a
much-delayed but triumphal visit, in May 1996. But in Bulgaria, too,
political sentiment for a restoration waned. Somehow, a monarchy
did not fit the image of a modern, Europe-focused Bulgaria. The
Tsar did return to politics – but as Simeon Saxecoburggotski, elected
prime minister in 2001. Thus national traditions took a back seat
to modern politics, and the former Tsar soon found his charisma
alone could not resolve his country's mundane problems. In both
cases, monarchist dreams could not fulfill the demands of modern
nationalism. Michael, Simeon, and their royal peers represented
their nations as political entities. They had little to say about their
nations as ethnic groups – and that version of nation is more powerful today.

It is hard to claim, though, that more traditional nationalists
have been any more successful. Every country in the region can
boast one or more extremist parties. Such parties call for expulsion of minorities, or for the expansion of borders (or both); they
have, so far, not come even close to attaining political power, except
in the war-torn former Yugoslav countries (where, in any case, it
becomes difficult to distinguish extremists from the mainstream).
Nevertheless, they have represented a serious test for new democracies, and an even greater test for civil society. Particularly where
civil liberties and minority rights are yet so fragile, extremism, even

on the margins, has been able to unsettle society, and pave the way for more palatable forms of extremism to take power.

The most prominent such figure outside the former Yugoslavia is probably Gheorghe Funar, of the Party of Romanian National Unity. His party was created by the ultra-nationalist movement "Romanian Hearth" in 1990; ex-communists looking for a new home dominated both. Funar, elected mayor of the Transylvanian city Cluj in February 1992, plays upon what Vladimir Tismaneanu calls "fantasies of redemption" – dreams of a return to national glory. His party, which he headed until ousted (after weak parliamentary election results) in November 1996, evokes memories of a Great Romania, brought low by foreigners – meaning both the capitalist, exploitative West and the Hungarians, Romanians' traditional adversary.[3] As mayor, Funar tried to prevent the display of the Hungarian flag by the Hungarian Consulate, denounced the visit to his city of Hungarian political leaders, banned the use of Hungarian on public signs (in defiance of national law), and had stray dogs painted in the colors of the Hungarian flag. All these have gained him national visibility but have not translated to widespread electoral support beyond Transylvania. After his ouster, Funar joined forces with another extremist, Corneliu Vadim Tudor, and his Greater Romania Party. Tudor began his career as Nicolae Ceaușescu's "court poet"; he exemplifies extremist nationalism's communist roots. Today, Tudor's rhetoric is the most antisemitic of that of any major politician in Eastern Europe. A particular target was Romania's first post-communist prime minister, Petre Roman, whom Tudor depicted as a part of a worldwide Jewish conspiracy.[4] Tudor and Funar's party won over 20 percent of the vote in parliamentary elections in 2000; subsequently, the party has tried to shed its extremist, antisemitic image. Funar came in a distant third in his bid for a fourth term as mayor, in 2004, and has faded from Romanian politics. Tudor shocked Romania by drawing 33 percent of the vote, coming in second in the 2000 presidential election, but has since seen his support dwindle.

The former anti-communist opposition has also furnished extremists. In many countries, figures once universally respected for their courage in facing communist repression now turn out to have little in common with their former dissident colleagues. One example is Hungarian playwright István Csurka. He helped mediate the rapprochement between reform communists and nationalist intellectuals in the mid-1980s, and was a founder of the Hungarian Democratic Forum (HDF), which led the country from 1990 to 1994. But in August 1992, Csurka published a lengthy essay describing an international conspiracy – of communists, Jews, and foreign capitalists, naturally – to weaken the only true Hungarian party. When the HDF belatedly expelled Csurka a year later, he formed the Hungarian Justice and Life Party, as a mouthpiece for his denunciations of the foreign control of Hungary. Csurka reached his pinnacle in 1998, when his party barely cleared the 5 percent hurdle to make it into Parliament; in recent years, it has retreated back to the fringe.

A third example, the most telegenic and perhaps most destructive of all, is the leader of the Czech Republican Party, Miroslav Sládek. Like other extreme nationalists, Sládek has a communist background: he worked as a censor. That has not prevented him from attacking national leaders for their communist pasts, and unmasking supposed agents of the former regime's secret police – President Havel was a favorite target. He too speaks of restoring glory to the Czech people, and identifying those (foreigners, Jews) responsible for hindering that destiny. More than have Csurka or Funar, Sládek has focused his venom on the most powerless: the Roma minority. This combination propelled the Republicans into Parliament in 1994, with 6 percent of the vote and fourteen seats, and increased its representation two years later.

It should be clear, though, that electoral support by itself is not a reliable measure of extremist nationalism. Simply the presence of a visible advocate of radical nationalism can have two effects. First, it can legitimize attacks on minorities within the country. A report from the Czech Ministry of Internal Affairs listed sixteen murders of Romas, and a total of 102 racially-motivated attacks in the years 1990–93 (presumably only a fraction of actual incidents); a party like Sládek's Republicans must bear some of the blame.[5] Second, such fringe politicians encourage mainstream leaders to echo their rhetoric. The willingness of leaders like Romanian President Ion Iliescu, or Hungarian Prime Minister József Antall, to espouse national chauvinist positions stems in part from their perception that they must appeal to that constituency. When Antall proclaimed that he was the leader of 15 million Hungarians – meaning the 10 million citizens of Hungary, plus the 5 million Hungarian minorities in neighboring countries (the actual number is probably closer to 3 million) for example, or when Iliescu allowed for veneration of figures associated with Romania's authoritarian past, they were treading paths cleared by the extremists.

Extremism's popularity, in other words, seems no greater than that of similar parties in Western Europe. The examples given here do not exhaust the phenomenon, of course. In those countries not consumed by war, nationalist extremism emerged in the early 1990s, when the novelty of democracy allowed for a radical diversity of views, and peaked in the mid-1990s, with the climax of uncertainties about economic success. They have generally declined dramatically, or transformed their message, since then. Today, a few are even deputies to the European Parliament in Strasbourg, where they have attempted to forge alliances with the likes of France's Le Pen. Rising prosperity and pro-European sentiments have made old-fashioned extremism even more marginal than it was.

On the other hand, new kinds of radicalism have emerged: In contemporary Eastern Europe, the Arab, Asian, or African refugee has replaced the Jew or other traditional minority as a scapegoat. While no East European country has witnessed attacks on refugees or guest workers approaching that observed in East Germany in the early 1990s,[6] fear of racial change has increased as borders have weakened. None of the countries of Eastern Europe, after all, has a past as a colonial power; refugees are therefore not the manifestation of imperial sins, but of the threat posed by globalization. The Arab on the city street, to many East Europeans, endangers national purity, and remains permanently outside the nation.

Minorities, majorities, citizens

That the modern state has the power to reduce or eliminate racial barriers was nicely illustrated by new Polish citizen Brian Scott, a popular talk-show host who had come to communist Poland from Guyana in 1985, when he displayed his identity card to viewers in 1998. Under the rubric "Distinguishing Marks," the document stated "none"; his race was bureaucratically invisible. But when I asked my Polish students in Wrocław whether Scott was therefore Polish, the answer was an emphatic, unanimous "no."

What does it mean to be Polish, or Latvian, or Macedonian in 2005? East European states have been undergoing an identity shift since 1989 – in fact, since the nineteenth century. In 1910, the majority of East Europeans lived in the multi-ethnic Russian, Ottoman, and Austro-Hungarian empires. World War One reordered the landscape, under the Wilsonian dictum of national self-determination. The new nation-states of Estonia, Latvia, Lithuania, and Poland were products of this idea. On the other hand, national self-determination had its limits: minority populations in the region included millions of Ukrainians, Hungarians, Jews, and Germans who were thus denied self-determination, while two states – Czecho-slovakia and Yugoslavia – had no majority nationality. The Wilsonian ideal could be blamed for much of the misfortune that has visited the region ever since. World War Two, and the cruel movement of populations after the war, were perverse but logical outcomes of the drive to allow any national group to be led by ethnic compatriots.

The communist regimes inherited societies much more homo-geneous than they had been before. Budapest, Prague, Riga, Vilnius, Warsaw, and many other lesser cities had been vibrantly multi-ethnic before World War Two. The Holocaust claimed most of their Jewish populations; only Hungary could still claim to have even a frac-tion of its prewar Jewish community. Some 10 million Germans in the Baltics, Czechoslovakia, Hungary, Poland, and Yugoslavia fled the advancing Soviet Army or were deported thereafter. Poland and Romania lost their multi-ethnic easts to the Soviet Union, to what would much later become independent Lithuania, Belarus, Ukraine, and Moldova. Deportations and border-drawing, in other words, gave communist states the gift of purity. Only Yugoslavia remained truly diverse, and continued, under Tito, to pursue the chimera of multi-ethnicity. The others worked to deepen national control: Poland and Romania, for example, expelled Jews (Romania even charged a hefty fee to Israel in the process), while Bulgarian communists tried to assimilate forcibly the Turkish minority there.

With the fall of communism, as national ideas appeared to return from the freezer, the question of minorities also returned. Minority rights was one of the severest tests facing the new democracies. Most failed that test at the outset; on balance, the record of post-communism has been terrible. While most nations did not even contemplate the genocide that was the fate of Bosnian Muslims, and that Kosovar Albanians narrowly averted, the experience of minorities throughout the region has been difficult.

There are three kinds of minority issues in Eastern Europe. The first concerns minorities that are labeled as powerful and threatening (whether or not they actually are, of course). These are primarily Jews, Germans, and Russians. Only Budapest still today has a sizeable Jewish community; in the entire region there are no more than a quarter-million Jews. Yet journalist Jonathan Kaufman writes in *A Hole in the Heart of the World* that he set out to write an "obituary about Jews in … Eastern Europe … [but] suddenly realized I was writing a birth announcement."[7] Indeed, signs of renaissance abound, in festivals of Jewish culture, in periodicals like the Warsaw monthly *Midrasz*, or in anecdotes about young adults converting to Judaism upon discovering roots hidden for half a century.

At the same time, antisemitic traditions die hard, even among those who are not entirely sure what a Jew is. The first two presidential campaigns in Poland featured insinuations that candidates were hiding Jewish backgrounds. In Croatia, Franjo Tudjman famously declared, in his successful campaign for the presidency in 1990: "Thank God, my wife is neither a Serb nor a Jew." Romanian newspapers have resurrected the blood libel. That none of these grotesque fantasies had anything to do with actual Jews is not the point. They feed fear, just as allusions to vampires or monsters might, but with an apparent rooting in reality. When Józef Cardinal Glemp, Primate of the Catholic Church in Poland, alluded to Jewish control of the international media during a conflict over Catholic symbols in and near the Auschwitz concentration camp, he provided a convenient, simple-minded answer to the problem of inferiority felt by many Poles, and East Europeans, after the euphoria of communism's fall subsided.[8]

If Jews function partly as myths in the East European mind, Germans, Turks, and Russians are quite real. Poland in particular has a large German minority, perhaps 800,000 strong, which is guaranteed seats in Parliament and language rights at the local level. The fear of Germans has rapidly mutated, however; Germans are no longer revanchist Nazis (that image is as likely to inspire admiration, on the extremist fringe, as it is fear), but represent the avaricious capitalist West, eager to buy up land and companies. Most recently, the Polish government has won a battle to deny Silesians – who occupy a kind of middle ground between Polish and German culture – the right to register as a national group, a step which might effectively have doubled or tripled the Germanic footprint in Poland.

Turks constitute about 10–12 percent of the population of Bulgaria; in 1984, communist leader Todor Zhivkov initiated a campaign to assimilate Turks, forcing them to slavicize their names; over 200,000 Turks fled or were expelled in the summer of 1989. The fact that these repressions came so late, and were so evidently an effort to pander to Bulgarian nationalism, perhaps accounts for the rapid reversal of discrimination policies in December 1989. Nationalist demonstrations against Turks were few and brief. Subsequently, Bulgaria has reached a conclusion similar to that of Poles regarding Germany: Turkey is an important ally, and there is nothing to be gained by antagonizing it. The Bulgarian Turks are also one of the few minority groups in Eastern Europe (the Hungarians of Slovakia are another) to develop a political party, the Movement for Rights and Freedoms, that has actually contributed to stabilizing, rather than unsettling, democracy.

Russians, a significant presence only in the Baltic states (as well as in the rest of the former Soviet Union) may be the most powerful minority in Eastern Europe. In Estonia and Latvia, they constitute nearly one-third of the population; the number in Lithuania is under 10 percent. Most moved into the Baltic republics during the communist period, as workers in new industries. Today, the Russian language is still ubiquitous in most Latvian cities, while the northeast corner of Estonia is almost entirely Russian. Given the small size of the Baltic nations (there are roughly one million ethnic Estonians, and 1.4 million Latvians) and their relatively short history of independence, it has been easy to see Russians as a genuine threat to the very survival of Estonian or Latvian language and culture. Thus, citizenship and language debates have dominated the politics of these two states since independence. Both countries have imposed strict language requirements for citizenship, meaning that many ethnic Russians find themselves essentially stateless. Only pressure from the Council of Europe, and then from the European Union, has prevented what some critics termed an "ethnic cleansing."[9] Nowhere outside the former Yugoslavia does the politics of ethnic survival carry so much weight.

If some minorities have been or are still feared, others, particularly the Roma, have traditionally been perceived as problems from below, as it were. Some 5 to 7 million Roma live in Eastern Europe, principally in Romania, Bulgaria, Hungary, Serbia and Montenegro, Slovakia, the Czech Republic, and Macedonia (in descending order). Once again, the communist regimes (and the Nazi genocide before that) laid the ground for contemporary attitudes. The semi-nomadic Roma have posed a problem for centralizing, modernizing states. Every regime forced the Roma to settle down; in Czechoslovakia, for example, many Roma were resettled in the less desirable cities of the Sudetenland after the Germans were expelled. They have remained at the margins of East European society, often unable to obtain even the documents necessary to join mainstream society. For other East Europeans experiencing the transition, and hoping to be accepted as "European," meanwhile, Roma have been a convenient target. In the first half of the 1990s, there were pogroms against Roma communities in Poland, Slovakia, the Czech Republic, Hungary, Romania, and Bulgaria. Roma experience vastly higher rates of unemployment, infectious diseases, and lack of education. As attitudes toward other minorities have changed, the prejudice against Roma remains respectable, equalled only by attitudes toward the still-small numbers of developing-world refugees. In October 1999, the North Bohemian town of Ústí nad Labem constructed a five-foot wall around two apartment blocks populated mostly by Roma. As the mayor explained: "the priority [is] the social demands of the town's citizens who obey the laws of the Czech Republic."[10] That a ghetto could return to the center of Europe sixty years after the Holocaust was grotesque. Some residents called for even stricter segregation, but the fence was dismantled the following year.

Shakespeare in Yugoslavia

Eastern Europe is no longer the multi-ethnic canvas it once was, but the diversity of cultures is greater than in most of Western Europe. The nation-state may not be the ideal form; in the twentieth century, however, it almost became ubiquitous in the developed world, ever since Woodrow Wilson arrived in Paris in 1919 with his gospel of national self-determination. As the Soviet Union, Yugoslavia, and Czechoslovakia broke up in 1991–93, Eastern Europe adopted the model of the Western nation-state; it was not suppressed nationalism, in other words, that resulted in genocide in Yugoslavia, but the lure of the nation-state. Most other nation-states in Europe were created through wars (of unification or disunification) and the violent destruction of empires. An optimist might observe that, just as 1989 showed that revolutionary change could be non-violent, so too the break-up of the Soviet Union and Czechoslovakia (to be considered later in this chapter) set a standard for the peaceful dissolution of multi-ethnic states. Yugoslavia's self-annihilation, though, suggests precisely the opposite.

The complicated story of Yugoslavia's break-up was a tragedy in five acts: prelude in Kosovo, the Slovene departure, the Croatian War, the Bosnian genocide, and the return to Kosovo. The Kosovar prelude, up until 1989, appeared to forecast destructive violence; ethnic divisiveness in Yugoslavia centered around this largely Muslim Albanian province. Though just 10 percent or fewer of its residents were Serb, the province had a strong hold on the Serb imagination, as the site of medieval Serb glory. To the rest of Yugoslavia, Kosovo was either a drain on federal coffers (as the poorest part of the country), a victim of Serb aggression, or both.

Demonstrations in Priština, Kosovo's capital, in 1981 had aroused the support of many across Yugoslavia; in response, Serbian intellectuals in the Academy of Sciences issued a memorandum in 1986 describing the fate of the dwindling Serb minority in Kosovo as "genocide" at the hands of Albanians. In April 1987, Slobodan Milošević made his now-famous visit to Kosovo; he entered as a dull communist official, secure in his position as President of the Serbian League of Communists, the second-highest position in the Serb party apparatus, and left a champion of the Serb national cause.

Confronted by Serb nationalists (who had staged a confrontation with police outside a meeting where Serbs voiced complaints of ethnic repression), Milošević uttered the ominous words: "No one will ever beat you again."[11] Two springs later, having already faced down party bosses in Vojvodina, another multi-ethnic province within Serbia, Milošević engineered a change in the Serb constitution, stripping Kosovo of its autonomy and subjecting it directly to Belgrade's rule. That history jumped the rails of logic into insanity is in large part the fault of one man and his ability to withstand or manipulate outside pressure as he pursued total political power.

Still, Yugoslavia was in 1989 rather similar to other multi-ethnic states in some ways, with a large constituency committed to the idea of "brotherhood and unity," the slogan at the heart of Josip Tito's vision. An opposite trend, leading toward a peaceful dissolution like that in the Soviet Union, could be discerned. Given that Yugoslavia was a modern state – no less so than was the Soviet Union – disintegration could have been an amiable, or at least orderly affair.

In Act Two, in 1990–91, the actors sought for an alternative path out of Yugoslavia. No Yugoslav republic feared Serb nationalism more than Slovenia. This is somewhat ironic, in hindsight, since Slovenia suffered least on its path to independence. Yet the strong civil society that had emerged there during the 1980s meant that Slovenes felt they had the most to lose. Unlike the rest of the country, Ljubljana already boasted a vibrant political life, ranging from nationalist discussion groups to feminist circles, as well as a weekly news magazine *Mladina* (Youth), which was the most daring in the country. The Slovene League of Communists had turned firmly reformist, heading in the direction already blazed in Hungary and Poland; other political parties were already making themselves heard. The June 1988 trial of four *Mladina* journalists for betraying military secrets had sparked endless protests directed against Belgrade; in February 1989, a huge rally in Ljubljana condemned Serb repression in Kosovo. It seemed the country was being torn between the two poles of ethnic repression and ethnic solidarity.

Even at that point, Yugoslavia was not doomed. One powerful institution still held Yugoslavia together: the League of Communists. The spirit of Tito was not entirely incompatible with the spirit of reform; indeed, Yugoslavia's long tradition of innovation in the dismal science of communist rule could surely have furnished reforms of which even Gorbachev would have been proud. Perhaps the problem was that communism in Yugoslavia had been too successful, and widely accepted. It was that much harder, then, for the communists to turn their back on their legacy, as leaders to the north would do that year. Moreover, reform (even of a Gorbachevian variety) would not happen in a vacuum. But except in Slovenia, society simply was inactive, and unable to exert from below any pressure for change.

That left nationalism. Quite simply, national pride became the distraction from the communist débâcle. As the Yugoslav economy spiraled in and out of chaos, leaders could have admitted that self-management, and all the other trappings of Yugoslav communism, had simply failed, and staged a round table to negotiate a transfer of power to liberal, democratic forces. Instead, Slobodan Milošević found it easier, and more conducive to his rise to power, to point the finger at Albanians, Slovenes, Croats, and Bosnians who persecuted Serbs. In so doing, he replaced the Titoist vision of brotherhood and unity with a vision of a Greater Serbia.

By 1990, the League of Communists was no longer Tito's party, but a raucously diverse political club only just barely displaying fealty to the "brotherhood and unity" ideal. Perhaps the League was doomed to fail, after a year of East European revolution. That was not yet evident when the Fourteenth Extraordinary Congress opened in Belgrade in January 1990. Angered by Serbian stonewalling, as Milošević and his allies defeated just about every proposal aimed toward liberalization, the Slovene delegation walked out on the third day. Serbian delegates applauded their departure, until the Croatian delegates followed suit, as they had promised. With this, the League of Communists – the main institution, along with the army, uniting Yugoslavia – effectively dissolved.

From this moment, Slovene exit from Yugoslavia was highly likely. In April 1990, Slovenia staged the first free election in postwar Yugoslavia; communist leader Milan Kučan (who had led the January walkout) was elected president, but a coalition of anti-communist parties, DEMOS, controlled Parliament. The Yugoslav Army (JNA) threatened retaliation for this nationalist vote, but the Slovenes had faced down the army before, in the demonstrations of 1988–89, and Kučan had a mandate for greater autonomy. He blocked JNA efforts to strip Slovene Territorial Defense units of weapons, and thus laid the foundations for a future Slovene Army. In December 1990, Slovenes voted overwhelmingly in favor of a referendum on independence. Over the next six months, the Slovenes carefully assembled all that a small independent country would need: police, border regulations, state insignia, etc. Not so long before, Slovene activists had sported half-humorous buttons referring to their then-meaningless border with Croatia: "When I grow up, I will be a customs officer on the Tolpa River." Now, it would come true.

For a seventy-year-old state, created originally as the "Kingdom of Serbs, Croats, and Slovenes," to come apart peacefully seemed improbable. Milošević, however, made it clear to Kučan that Serbia would not thwart Slovenia's secession; there were, after all, no Serbs in Slovenia. Yet when the Slovene Parliament almost unanimously declared independence on June 25, 1991, the JNA began what it described as a "police action," with fewer than 2,000 troops. Slovenia responded with force, and declared war.[12] Within three days, Milošević and his allies decided that, after all, Slovenia was not worth fighting for. It took European Community negotiators a further week to reach the same conclusion that Yugoslavia no longer existed, in a pact signed on the Adriatic island of Brioni.

The Slovene war spelled the end of a federal Yugoslavia, already weakened by a decade of growing national conflict. Its resolution made it possible to envision that other republics could also secede. Act Three of the Yugoslav drama would be quite different. Now that the ideals of Yugoslav unity were negated, the only question left was that of national supremacy within Yugoslavia and, given the devolution of power to the republics since Tito's death, within each of them as well. To Belgrade, it was always clear that what applied to Slovenia could not possibly apply to Croatia. Some 10 percent of Croatia's population was ethnically Serb, mostly settled in Eastern Slavonia, on the border with Serbia, and in the Krajina region bordering Bosnia-Hercegovina. Croatian secession thus had entirely different implications.

The Croatian war would be a battle of nationalisms. The Croatian path toward independence was radically different from that of Slovenia. Many Croatian leaders, including President Franjo Tudjman, had cut their teeth in the "Croatian Spring" of 1971. Expelled from the League of Communists and imprisoned for his nationalist heresy, Tudjman had spent the 1980s networking with Croatian émigrés in Canada, Australia, and the United States. For them, there could be no compromise on Croatian identity; Tudjman (who had fought in Tito's Partisan Army in World War Two) showed what he had learned when he revived the symbols of Croatia's wartime fascist state, in particular the checkerboard flag (the *Šahovnica*) that, to Serbs, symbolized the bloody, even genocidal, regime that had claimed the lives of hundreds of thousands of Serbs fifty years before. Had Tudjman proclaimed that his Croatia would honor the Titoist ideals of national coexistence (or embraced a democratic version of the same), perhaps war would have been avoided. Yet non-Croats were required to show that they had proficiency in Croatian, while automatic citizenship (and the right to vote) was extended to Croatian émigrés everywhere; the constitution described Serbs as a "national minority." Krajina Serbs formed a political party, and, with backing from Belgrade, asserted more and more control over their region. When Croatia declared independence, it could not claim to be in command of its own territory.

Beginning in July 1991, Serb paramilitaries and the JNA conducted assaults on Croat-held territory in and around the Krajina; in August began the assault on Eastern Slavonia. The siege of Vukovar, the largest city of Eastern Slavonia, which lasted from September to November 1991, was one of the cruelest chapters in the Yugoslav wars. As they would again in Bosnia, the victorious Serbs separated captured Croatian men – including hundreds of wounded from the Vukovar hospital – from women and children. The men were executed, and buried in a mass grave outside the city.

The war in Croatia came uneasily to a halt at the end of 1991. The European Community had attempted to impose criteria on Yugoslav republics wishing to be recognized as independent. Germany's Chancellor Helmut Kohl derailed this by announcing in December that his country would recognize both Slovenia and Croatia. Though Franjo Tudjman could not claim control over fully one-third of the country – and though the early stages of the war had nearly cost him his career – his vision of Croatia as a uni-ethnic state had prevailed, and his Croatian Democratic Union would exert a stranglehold over national politics for the rest of the decade. In August 1995, as the war in Bosnia was reaching its last frenzied stage, Tudjman launched "Operation Storm," in which a rejuvenated Croatian Army recaptured the Krajina region in a matter of days. Croatian nationalism was still on the offensive: in an election called shortly afterwards, twelve seats in Parliament represented Croats living abroad – mostly in Bosnia-Hercegovina. Though most had never lived in Croatia, the implication was that Croatia would soon come to them.

The third act of the tragedy had demonstrated that logics of state power would give way to nationalist power. In Act Four – often seen as a culmination of "ancient ethnic hatreds" – history would be completely abandoned in a drive for political control. Determining the meaning of ethnicity in the Yugoslav wars is in fact difficult. True, one can make rather too much of the fact that the first JNA soldier killed in the Slovene war was himself Slovene, as was the coordinator of JNA forces in Zagreb; that the mayor of Vukovar was a Serb; and that a member of Milošević's security detail would later lead a Muslim uprising in Srebrenica. Yet there is no doubt that, by 1990, most people had become more or less comfortable as citizens of Yugoslavia. In an increasingly urbanized society, ethnic ties were fragmenting, not deepening, while religious affiliation was weakening. On the other hand, Yugoslavia was not just any multi-ethnic federal state; for fully sixty years – since a Montenegrin Serb had shot and killed the leading Croat politician during a parliamentary debate – it had lacked the forms of democracy which might have subordinated existing ethnic differences to political ones. As civil society did take shape, it was as likely to vocalize ethnic demands as not. In the end, though, while the exploration of ethnopolitics was inevitable as communism crumbled, war and genocide were not.

Bosnia was in some ways a microcosm of Yugoslavia. Its 4 million inhabitants were Bosnian Muslim, Serb, and Croat. The Muslim inhabitants – Slavs whose ancestors had converted to Islam in the fifteenth century, and who were thus indistinguishable from their Christian neighbors except by name – were largely secular; in Mostar in 1995, a Bosnian economist commented wistfully to me that if one more generation had been allowed to live in peace, even the pseudo-ethnic differences would have disappeared, as there were fewer and fewer observant Muslims; he saw parallels with the assimilated Jews of Weimar Germany. Many factors made war likely, chiefly the activities and the blunders of a few political leaders within Bosnia and without. Culture was not one of them.

Perhaps the key to Bosnian disintegration, in the end, was the *ključ* (key), the Titoist rotational system that delicately balanced each ethnicity against each other – in the rotating federal presidency (and the corresponding Bosnian presidency), in the military's officer corps, in bureaucratic appointments, even in favors and repressions dispensed from Belgrade. Instead of defusing ethnicity, the *ključ* politicized it, placing a zero-sum ethnic contest at the center of politics. And where Slovenia had an active civil society, and Croatia had its nationalist Croatian Spring, the Bosnians had only the latent competition among the national triad. In 1990, each of the three groups formed nationalist parties, which dominated the election of November 1990. In the terms laid down by Milošević, by Tudjman, and indeed by Western negotiators, it became difficult to imagine a non-nationalist politics. Bosnian President Alija Izetbegović spoke of the one-man, one-vote principle, which would mean a slight Muslim dominance; his Serb counterpart Radovan Karadzić, leader of the Serbian Democratic Party, played upon fears of an Islamic Republic. In a chilling speech to the Parliament on October 14, 1991, Karadzić essentially promised obliteration of the Muslims and Bosnia: "Do not think that you will not perhaps make the Muslim people disappear, because the Muslims cannot defend themselves if there is war. How will you prevent everyone from being killed in Bosnia-Hercegovina?"[13] The Serb delegates subsequently quit Parliament, forming their own separatist Parliament in a Sarajevo suburb. When President Izetbegović called a referendum on Bosnian independence a few months later, Serbs boycotted the vote.

On April 6, 1992, the European Community recognized Bosnia as an independent state. That same week, Serb forces – JNA troops, Serbian police units, and Bosnian Serb paramilitaries – began ethnically cleansing towns near the Serbian border. This meant surrounding a town, issuing an ultimatum to all Muslims to surrender, followed by a massive invasion and a house-to-house search. The invaders massacred those who had not left, or forced them to flee their homes with few or no possessions. Often they came with lists of prominent Muslims, who were taken away and executed. Soon, Serb forces created concentration camps, most infamously at Omarska and Keraterm.

But in Sarajevo, people believed there was a different Bosnia, one that rose above nationalism. To them, the danger was from provincial, backward Bosnia, which could not destroy the modern, tolerant society that flourished in the capital (and in a few other cities). A peace demonstration on April 5, 1992, attracted thousands of Sarajevans from all nationalities; Serb paramilitaries fired on the crowd, killing one. Soon, Sarajevo would be at the very center of the war, isolated from the world and subject to daily bombard-ments from the surrounding hills, its most beautiful monuments destroyed. Sarajevo became both a symbol of Bosnian hope and of its humiliation, as well as of the callous inhumanity of a war in which civilians – darting across Sniper's Alley in search of water, standing in breadlines, or simply sitting at home – were the main targets.

Many dimensions of the Bosnian horror – cattle cars, barbed wire, and mass graves; guards given free rein to exercise their most sadistic impulses; the open rhetoric about racial superiority; the destruction of assimilated and tolerant communities, beginning with community leaders – bring to mind the Holocaust. The Bosnian war, in which 200,000–250,000 died and more than 2 million became refugees, was indeed the Holocaust's successor, the first genocide on European soil in forty-seven years. As in Hitler's Final Solution, the refugees and the civilian deaths were not simply a byproduct of the war, but its purpose. If Wilsonian national self-determination was the goal, then only through ethnic cleansing – a term that entered our lexi-con through the Yugoslav wars – could ethnically rational lines (like that between Slovenia and Croatia) be drawn on the Bosnian map to separate nations so that they might be self-governed.

In the 1990s, however, total physical extermination was unnec-essary in order to achieve this goal (nor, it should be clear, is it necessary in order that we may use the term "genocide"). The Serbs added new weapons to the genocidal arsenal. First, humiliation and harassment – for example, being forbidden to work, to drive cars, to use telephones – drove thousands to flee their homes. The Nazis had employed similar schemes, but in Bosnia these provoked rapid self-cleansing. Second, the Serbs enlisted the peacekeeping forces as unwilling allies. Early on in the war, they discovered that UN forces could even be induced to provide the buses and the logistics for the ethnic cleansing. Later, when Western resolve appeared to harden, they turned peacekeepers into hostages, chaining them to military installation fences to thwart bombing runs, and so ethnic cleansing could continue. And third, they used the small scope of the war to their advantage; soon the West had its hands full with refugees, leaving little room to focus on the crime of ethnic cleansing itself.

Serb paramilitaries visited terrible humiliation upon the women of Bosnia. Rape had of course been a part of war before – most notably at the end of World War Two, when Soviet soldiers raped thousands of German women – but in Bosnia, the victims were not members of a defeated nation; nor was rape inseparable from looting. Carried out in the camps and police stations of Bosnia, these mass rapes manipulated ideas of honor and nationalism to, in effect, remove the women from the Bosnian Muslim community. The negation of reproduction – by the killing of men in a community, or by the emotional and physical scarring of women – could have the same effect as total physical liquidation, especially if survivors could be made to disappear, or to retreat to an ethnic enclave.[14]

In the late summer of 1992, the Bosnian war acquired a new dimension, becoming a three-cornered war. Until then, many Bosnian Croats (who had seen their national kin ethnically cleansed in Vukovar and the Krajina) assumed that they had a common fight against Serb ethnic cleansing. Franjo Tudjman had encouraged the Croats of Hercegovina to see themselves as part of an ethnic Croatian state. His man in Hercegovina, Mate Boban, announced the creation of an ill-defined "Croatian Community of Herceg-Bosna," in which the "Croatian language" was spoken. (Nothing shows the absurdity of national conflict in Bosnia better than language. Serbs, Muslims, and Croats spoke essentially the same language until the war, differing mainly in the use of either the Cyrillic or Latin alphabets.

Subsequently, the Croatian media daily promoted Croatian neo-logisms – sometimes derived from medieval Croatian texts – while some Bosnian Muslims began to greet each other with *"Salaam"* instead of *"Dobar dan."*) Months of small-scale ethnic cleansing of Muslims led to open war in April 1993. By that summer, the Croats of Hercegovina could boast a camp system almost as grim as that of the Serbs. In November, Croat gunners with nothing better to do destroyed the sixteenth-century footbridge at Mostar.

A sense of absurdity hung above the conflict. It sometimes looked as if Yugoslavia would end up producing well more than just six separate countries. Sarajevans published a tongue-in-cheek "Sara-jevo Survival Guide," teaching would-be tourists how to scavenge for firewood or to get by on ersatz coffee. Sarajevans also took an ironic perspective on the brief solidarity shown by Western politicians or cultural figures who dropped in from time to time, and whose visits had little effect. The greatest source of absurdity was the presence of hapless peacekeeping forces from the UN unable to protect anyone from ethnic cleansing, and often going to great lengths to ensure that the process went smoothly. Yet if sometimes the conflict seemed nothing but a dark comedy of Balkan folly, it was anything but. Some 10,000 people died in Sarajevo alone. Complex societies harboring simple ideas of coexistence (if not love) were thoroughly destroyed, along with the monuments of their cultures. Bosnia did not become uni-ethnic, but it did become soaked with national chauvinism – an ideology singularly lacking in humor.

Another myth about the Bosnian war – fostered by reminders that Karadzić was a psychiatrist, Boban a furniture-store owner, etc. – is that the war was the product of ill-trained bands of amateur fighters, clumsily enacting the dictates of their fanatical leaders. The genocide at Srebrenica, one of the final acts of the Bosnian war, puts the lie to that delusion. Srebrenica was one of several UN "safe areas," enclaves of Muslims in Eastern Bosnia ostensibly protected by UN forces. The assault against them was led by Gen-eral Ratko Mladić, Commander of the Bosnian Serb Army. By July 1995, Muslim refugees had swelled Srebrenica to some 40,000, five times its prewar size. Quickly overrunning the frightened Dutch peacekeepers, Mladić's troops were able to take the town without difficulty. Mladić assured the townspeople that no harm would come to them. But those who had not fled into the mine-infested forests for the long trek to almost unattainable safety faced a terrible fate. Women and children were ethnically cleansed, on buses provided by the UN. Some 7,000 men and boys were herded into the soccer stadium, into schoolyards, and factory warehouses around the town, and executed.

There was no way for Western observers to parse this atrocity: it was genocide. Srebrenica did not end the war, though – and, worse, the Bosnian Serb Republic would soon be awarded control of that cleansed city. Barely three weeks after Srebrenica, Tudjman launched Operation Storm; at the same time, the Bosnian Army, now once again fighting alongside the Croats, began to push back its Serb opponents everywhere. Milošević, whose ambitions had always been stretched beyond Greater Serbia to world recognition, reached the conclusion that the Bosnian Serbs and the Krajina Serbs were now a liability, and that national unification could not succeed. Tens of thousands of expelled Serbs streamed across Serb-controlled Bosnia toward Serbia proper, while the Bosnian Serb Army fell back in disarray.

It was time for the war to end. Fearing that a refugee crisis would destabilize Serbia, the Americans arranged for "proximity talks" – in which Milošević (representing the Bosnian Serbs, whom he cut out of the negotiations), Izetbegović, and Tudjman bargained through their hosts, principally Assistant Secretary of State Richard Holbrooke, in order to draw an acceptable map of Bosnia. The talks took place at Wright-Patterson Air Force Base in Dayton, Ohio, in November 1995. There, the ethnic cleansing continued: each side traded away towns and villages under its control, while the very discussions imputed national designations – this town is Serb, that one is Muslim – to places that had been fully multi-ethnic just three years earlier. But all recognized (for different reasons) that violent ethnic cleansing would no longer bring returns. In accordance with ground rules laid out at the beginning of the talks, the Muslim–Croat federation would control 51 percent of the territory to the Serb Republic's 49 percent. The convoluted internal borders that resulted did not make Bosnia seem any more a country than before; indeed, the NATO occupation of Bosnia would continue for nearly a decade, until the European Union took over in early 2005.

As with all other negotiations in that decade, it seemed to the Americans that they had solved Yugoslavia's ethnic problems with some elegant line-drawing and some maneuvers to protect politicians' dignity. Yet democracy-building commitments at Dayton would mostly be neglected in the rush to administer ethnic categories. The Americans (and other Western leaders) felt they understood the Yugoslavs when they penetrated politics to get to nationalism, when in fact it was the other way around: under nationalist demands was the bedrock of political calculation. The main actors were determined to keep the drama going. Milošević had given up on his idea of Greater Serbia, but he would still be ready to defend his idea of Serbia (and what was still then called Yugoslavia) itself. And one group in particular was ignored at Dayton, and would come back on stage in Act Five: the Kosovar Albanians.

Kosovo was not Bosnia. Albanians and Serbs were not close to one another, generally did not intermarry, and spoke mutually incomprehensible languages. (The name, too, is hotly debated; British peace activists combined the Serb "o" and the Albanian "a" into "Kosov@.") National difference was here rather more than politics, even if many Serb grievances (such as those in the 1986 Memorandum) were invented. Kosovars faced a powerful foe in Serbia; for nearly eight years after the province lost its autonomy (in 1989), the Kosovar strategy was straight from the pages of underground Central Europe. Their goal was simply cultural survival, led by their president (elected by underground ballot) Ibrahim Rugova. An underground educational system stretched across Kosovo, as did an underground press. Polish journalist Konstanty Gebert recounted to me his surprise upon discovering, a few years earlier, that Kosovars were teaching their children from Serbian history textbooks. Why don't you print your own? he asked, and couldn't understand why lack of a printing press would be a problem. With a few boards, some cloth, and some elastic ripped from underwear, he demonstrated how he had printed underground Solidarity periodicals during Poland's martial law in the 1980s. A year later, his Albanian friends proudly presented him with a new history text, fresh off an underground Kosovar press.

Dayton was a brutal awakening; it seemed as if Kosovo had been left to the mercy of Serbia, and that the West was finished exacting good behavior from Milošević. Years of Rugova's moderation had not paid off. The tiny Kosovo Liberation Army (KLA) proposed a violent alternative. It grew rapidly, especially after the post-pyramid anarchy in Albania made arms easily available. In early 1997, it staged its first small attacks – mostly on Serb policemen relaxing in cafés. The response was predictable: Serbia launched a "scorched-earth campaign"[15] against Albanian opposition of any kind, militants and moderates alike. It should have come as no surprise, given recent trends, that this culminated in the first reports of genocidal massacres, most famously at Račak, in January 1999, where forty-five villagers were murdered.

What happened next can broadly be summed up thus: the world had, astoundingly, learned from its mistakes. Kosovo did not become another Bosnia. Western allies (and Russia) convened a conference at Rambouillet near Paris, in February–March. This was not a negotiation as at Dayton, but a means to deliver an ultimatum, establishing far-reaching autonomy within Yugoslavia, to Milošević (as well as to Albanian militants). Milošević refused to sign and, within days, NATO began a massive bombing campaign against Yugoslav Army forces in Kosovo and in Serbia proper. In a mockery of the air campaign, Milošević's forces began "Operation Horseshoe," intended to cleanse Kosovo of Albanians once and for all. Village after village was emptied at gunpoint and burned to the ground; thousands were killed, and endless columns of refugees made their way toward the borders with Macedonia or Albania. This strategy had worked before, when UN peacekeepers bussed Bosnian Muslims from their homes. As bombs hit refugee caravans and Belgrade civilians, not to mention the Chinese Embassy, it was easy to lose sight of the purpose of the war: to prevent yet another genocide. That goal was achieved when Milošević capitulated in early June.

Alternatives to cleansing

Like Bosnia, Kosovo cannot be put back together again. Serbs became the new refugees as vengeful Kosovar Albanians returned home. Similarly, Bosnian Muslims returning home either find large

angry crowds waiting to stone their buses, or confront the complicated prospect of evicting Serb settlers just as they were evicted. Wars
are not a way to restore society, multi-ethnic or otherwise, and the
smallest acts of violence will continue to inflame local passions. One
obstacle to peace is the memory that war creates, as will be discussed
in the next chapter. But the contrasts between the Bosnian and
Kosovo wars – between facilitating ethnic cleansing and stopping
it, between pretending that all sides were guilty and intervening
against an aggressor – shows us that national chauvinism is neither
inevitable nor unstoppable, even in Eastern Europe.

Other contrasts can also help us to pinpoint what is different
about the Yugoslav wars, as two other states broke up at the same
time as did Yugoslavia. The Baltic republics might appear on
the surface to have been as prone to conflagration as Yugoslavia.
Guerrilla warfare had continued in some parts until the late 1950s,
almost twenty years after the Soviet Union first invaded. The Russians, for their part, had learned about "Baltic fascism" from their
schoolbooks. Lithuania, followed shortly by its neighbors, declared
independence from the Soviet Union in March 1990, to no avail at
first, as the West studiously ignored it. Yet civil war did not follow.
There was plenty of combustible material; and on several occasions
there were explosions, most tragically when Soviet troops attacked
demonstrators by the television tower in Vilnius in January 1991,
killing fourteen. Two differences were key: first, the Russians in
the Baltics were not mobilized like the Serbs in Croatia, Bosnia,
or Kosovo. Soviet leaders had been no more willing to allow for
Russian national activism on the border than Estonian, Latvian,
or Lithuanian nationalism. Second, Mikhail Gorbachev never made
the switch that Slobodan Milošević did, from communist bureau-
crat to nationalist orator, though he certainly could have. This may
be Gorbachev's greatest achievement: the peaceful dissolution of
a multi-ethnic state, in the last days of 1991, while Milošević contrived to destroy everything he set his hand to, including the Serb
nation itself.

The dissolution of Czechoslovakia provides a poor comparison
to the other two. True, a multi-ethnic federal state sundered into
two. Here as well, political leaders contrived to divide the spoils

among themselves, in the name of national grievance. But in Czecho-slovakia, the decisions were so obviously cynical, without any serious appeal to popular desire, that national mobilization – let alone vio-lence – would have seemed preposterous. This is not to suggest, however, that Czechs and Slovaks did not have reason to seek what came to be known as the "Velvet Divorce."

The simplest explanation of the split between the Czechs and Slovaks, creating two separate states on January 1, 1993, is that, like the fall of Yugoslavia, it had much less to do with nationalism than with political manipulation. Indeed, while the Croats, Serbs, Bosnian Muslims, and Kosovar Albanians could point to bloody moments in their past – from the fourteenth century through World War Two – that implicated their national opponent, the Czechs and Slovaks had no such history. Quite the opposite: In the Habsburg Empire, the Czechs had vied for control of Prague with their German neighbors and fought for autonomy in Vienna, while Slovaks had to contend with Hungarian domination. Fear of Magyar cultural absorption and military aggression (as well as the earnest efforts of some political and cultural figures in both nations, including future Czechoslovak President Tomáš Masaryk) had driven Slovaks together with Czechs in 1918. In the subsequent seventy years together in one state, it is notable that Czechs and Slovaks never fought together against a common enemy, nor defended one another.[16] Moreover, the central-ization of power in the largest Czech city, though ameliorated some-what after 1968, heightened a sense in Bratislava that Slovakia might be better off alone. The communist policy of locating many major heavy industry plants, arms factories in particular, in Slovakia gave a false sense of self-sufficiency. (Interestingly, Bosnia industrialized in the same way under communism; economic concerns did not, however, play much of a role in the conflict there.)

Had accession to the European Union been on the immediate horizon in the early 1990s, or had hero of 1968 Alexander Dubček (a Slovak) been chosen to lead the united post-communist government, it is quite possible that Czechoslovakia would not have split in two. As it was, the euphoria of the Velvet Revolution quickly gave way to what seemed at first to be petty score-settling. When President Václav Havel proposed changing the country's name to the Czechoslovak

Republic (simply removing "Socialist" and returning to the pre-communist name), Slovaks objected to their continued lexicographic subordination. The so-called "hyphen war," over how to represent the Czech(o)-Slovak relationship, ensued. Having finally agreed upon a Czech and Slovak Federal Republic, however, politicians had no strength left to approve a constitution.

Economic factors contributed to the tension. Those arms factories and steel mills, once the pride of Slovakia, began to look like an albatross instead. On the one hand, Slovaks pointed to the environmental damage they had suffered thanks to policies crafted in Prague. On the other, the rapid decline of arms exports and military production – thanks to shock therapy and the moral concerns of former dissidents – threatened the livelihood of tens of thousands of Slovak workers. A group of Slovak economists in 1991 called for a rethinking of the federation, so as to guarantee each republic's "full economic sovereignty," warning that if Slovakia could not claim "its natural right to decide about its own economic fate," then it could not remain within the Czechoslovak state.[17]

Czechs and Slovaks quickly lost enthusiasm for their anti-communist leaders. In March 1991 Havel unexpectedly appeared at a rally in Bratislava, held to celebrate the anniversary of the founding of the Slovak fascist state during World War Two. An angry crowd booed the President, yelled "Judas"!, scuffled with his entourage, and spat on his car. Havel was effectively no longer in control of the state with whose liberation he had been so strongly identified in the West. He had lost his place to Václav Klaus, who saw federation with the Slovaks in purely practical terms, and determined that Slovakia hindered the Czech journey toward the free market and toward Europe. Meanwhile, the main revolutionary movement in Slovakia, Public Against Violence, split in two, over charges that it did not faithfully reflect Slovak interests. Prime Minister Vladimír Mečiar – a lawyer with a questionable communist past, but with great political skill – led the creation of the Movement for a Democratic Slovakia. Like Milošević, Mečiar was not known for his nationalism until late in the game, but proved to be quite flexible ideologically.[18] One month later, Mečiar was forced out of office; this move probably helped to radicalize Slovak nationalism, too.

An independent Slovakia did not have to happen, and few, until 1992, really expected that it would. A poll in September 1991 found that just 23 percent of Slovaks (and 13 percent of Czechs) supported a complete split, though a majority in Slovakia did perceive political and economic inequities. Nearly two-thirds in both republics agreed that "politicians are using the question of nationalism for their own purposes."[19] In June 1992, however, Czechs and Slovaks voted for the parties of politicians (Mečiar and Klaus) who favored, or at least did not oppose, a split. Without a national constitution, these leaders were free to go beyond what anyone expected, and divide the state. Over the summer, they signed agreements to do just this; almost before anyone realized it, and despite some last-minute Slovak cold feet, Czechoslovakia came to an end.

Compared to the demise of Yugoslavia, this was of course a "velvet" solution. The treatment of Roma and of other minorities since independence – such as Slovak efforts to ban the use of bilingual signs, or attempts to ignore less-proud moments of the past, as will be discussed in the next chapter – should warn us away from a neat contrast between "good" and "bad" nationalisms on a Central Europe–Balkan axis. As a final example of the development and use of nationalism in the post-communist world, we turn to Macedonia, where ethnic cleansing fortunately failed.

Other than Bosnia-Hercegovina, no state in the 1990s with poorer prospects for survival than Macedonia. Only in Bosnia, Estonia and Latvia are minority populations as large: fully 35 percent of Macedonia's 2 million residents, chiefly Albanian (25 percent). Macedonia also has the misfortune of strongly nationalist neighbors. Bulgaria has historically questioned whether a Macedonian nation even exists, and this claim resurfaced in Sofia in 1990. Yet while Macedonians developed a modern national identity only under Tito, hardly any today identify themselves as Bulgarian. Like Bosnian-Serbian-Croatian, Bulgarian and Macedonian are very similar; the Macedonian prime minister, however, made a point of using an interpreter during his Bulgarian counterpart's first state visit to Skopje in 1993.[20] To the south, Greece has regarded the very name "Macedonia," and the state flag which uses an emblem traced to Alexander the Great, as indicating designs on Greek Macedonia.

Since its independence, the state has had to use the official name "Former Yugoslav Republic of Macedonia" (FYROM). To the north is predatory Serbia, and to the east, Albania. It seemed entirely plausible that Macedonia might be partitioned among its neighbors.

The greatest threat to Macedonian stability, however, was from within. Fear of a bloody Slav–Albanian conflict appeared to be a self-fulfilling prophecy. In 1997, the Mayor of Gostivar received a thirteen-year sentence (he was amnestied in late 1998) for ordering the Albanian flag to be flown. Neighborhoods and playgrounds divided, and riots accompanied the opening of an underground Albanian-language university in Tetovo in 1995. As the KLA flexed its muscles to the north, it announced its presence in Macedonia, too, claiming credit for a series of bombs in several cities in 1998. The Kosovo war in March 1999 severely tested Macedonia, as over 300,000 refugees streamed across the border. It was a surprise to no one when armed conflict on a larger scale did erupt, finally, in early 2001. Soon, much of the area around Tetovo was under the control of the KLA. All that was missing to launch a full-scale ethnic conflagration was resentment of Western intervention, and sure enough, ethnic Macedonians began to perceive that European negotiators were favoring ethnic Albanian positions. When the Macedonian Army tried to retake a KLA-occupied town near Skopje in late June, NATO forces evacuated the rebels (and their weapons); Macedonian protesters stormed the parliament building, and later attacked Western embassies and the offices of foreign companies. The moment was ripe for a nationalist leader to rip apart Macedonia.

Several factors helped Macedonia avoid this terrible fate. First, Macedonia was simply too weak for such a move. The rebels, supported from Kosovo and Albania, were the ones with the arms and the momentum. While weakness has not stopped chauvinist demagogues from seizing power elsewhere, Macedonia (second) could not count on the benevolence of European leaders, as could, for example, Franjo Tudjman's Croatia. Third, for the first seven years of independence, Macedonia was not dominated by national parties. Instead, an ostensibly supra-national Social Democratic Party, led by Titoist Kiro Gligorov, continued to win elections while not ethnicizing itself as did Milošević's Social Democrats. Indeed, Gligorov tried to avoid the fate of his neighbors by requesting, in 1992, a UN force (UNPREDEP), which remained in Macedonia until China vetoed its renewal in 1999. As UNPREDEP head Henryk Sokalski boasts, this Preventive Deployment Force, present *before* conflict began, was able to keep ethnic opponents in contact with one another.[21]

Macedonia in the 1990s seemed rather like the old Yugoslavia, and was indeed not much more democratic. But as a result, nationalist politics was also framed as anti-communist, about lack of democracy and economic difficulties as much as national pride. When the nationalist party Internal Macedonia Revolutionary Organization-Democratic Party of Macedonian National Unity won the parliamentary election in October 1998, it surprised everyone by proposing a coalition with the most nationalist Albanian party, the Democratic Party of Albanians. This grand coalition became even grander during the 2001 unrest, as a new government that included virtually all the major parties sought a resolution. Thus political allegiances were more than just national, and Macedonia turned away from its worst impulses. An agreement in August 2001 gave the Albanian minority new constitutional rights (such as official-language status), and more local self-government, while disarming the rebels.

Perhaps Macedonia's success is only relative; after all, a NATO mission certainly helped to maintain peace. Terrorist bombings, sometimes credited to a new group called the Albanian National Army, show that the potential for ethnic conflict is still there. But the Macedonian example – as well as others discussed in this chapter, such as relations between Bulgarians and Turks, Czechs and Roma, or Latvians and Russians – reminds us that the key to national stability is not simply prosperity, nor even relative homogeneity. More essential are the ability to manage or come to terms with the past, and the depth of political society, to which we will turn in the next two chapters.

3 | Peeling away the past: nostalgia and punishment

Is there a country whose people are fully aware of and comfortable with their history? If so, historians would be out of work. Some states around the world are now grappling (with greater or lesser honesty) with the complexities of their pasts – the unacknowledged crimes, the hidden shames, the tarnished heroes – while others have not yet faced these questions. Democracies, where the press and historians are relatively unhindered, tend to fall into the former category; in undemocratic societies, such discussions are at the margins or underground, at best.[1]

Attention to the past has, for a variety of reasons, emerged most strongly in the last twenty years. In part, this is because of the very phenomenon that underpins this book: the fall of communism and the end of the Cold War. The disappearance of the two-camp division removed some of the reasons for silence: now, examination of one's own sins does not necessarily mean one is aiding the enemy. Second, the end of a war, even a cold one, invites examination of its crimes and its memory holes. This has also allowed for examination of aspects of the Holocaust that had been inaccessible until now.

There are other reasons, too. Democratization, whether or not it is an inevitable process, has touched many countries beyond the former Soviet bloc: the former dictatorships of the Mediterranean, Latin America, East and Southeast Asia, and Africa have also come under scrutiny. The growth of new social movements, organized around identity politics and protesting the ill-treatment of disadvantaged groups (women and minorities in particular), has put many misdeeds of the past on the political agenda. Human rights organizations (such as Amnesty International) and international agreements (like the Helsinki Accords) have gradually raised awareness, too. Simultaneously, the ongoing departure of the World War

Two/Holocaust generation has raised the urgency of coming to terms with the past. For all these reasons, there has never been such a focus on recent history as there is today.[2]

But so what? Why does this reassessment of the past matter to those who are not historians? While the phrase "come to terms with the past" may suggest a private struggle with memory, we are only now beginning to realize that there is some relationship between knowledge of the past and practices of the present. In which direction that relationship goes is less clear. On the one hand, societies that remember and acknowledge their pasts may be more successful at democracy, and may accord more freedoms to all. Yet, surely one can be too obsessed with the past, and with retribution or restitution. Post-communist Eastern Europe has been a laboratory for all kinds of memory. As we peel away layers of the past, moving from the recent horrors of the Yugoslav wars to the still-open wounds of World War Two, we will see how these stories affect East European attempts at democratic politics and their conceptions of their place in the world. Such an archaeological dig may suggest where the limits of memory should be, and whether there can also be benefits to forgetting or of accepting divergent memories.

Layer one: post-communist crimes

To begin with the obvious: None of the countries of Eastern Europe existed in the form they do today just a century ago. They have all been birthed, shaped, reshaped, or cleansed by the painful wars of the twentieth century. Most East European societies can find in those moments stories of great pride; they can also find, as they confront their pasts, that their future as well as their past rests upon shaky foundations. There is no better example today than Croatia. As we saw in the previous chapter, Croatia after its 1991 independence was both one of the first victims of the Yugoslav wars and complicit in some of the worst crimes of those conflicts. Today, Croatia's economy is booming, as tourism has returned stronger than ever. A half-decade after founder Franjo Tudjman's death, democracy appears strong, and the country is a clear third in line to join the European Union (after Bulgaria and Romania). One thing – aside from crises in the EU itself – stood in its way: the arrest of General Ante Gotovina.

Ante Gotovina is accused by the International Criminal Tribunal for the Former Yugoslavia (ICTY) of crimes committed during the liberation of Krajina from Serb forces in August 1995, in Operation Storm. Specifically, he is charged with causing the deaths of some 150 civilians, as well as the looting and destruction of Serb homes, with the intent to prevent refugees from returning to Croatia. These crimes are not so different from those committed by other military leaders, Croats included, in Bosnia. But Operation Storm is different: Not only to Croats, but to most observers around the world, it was a well-justified retaliation against Belgrade-supported Serb forces that had brutally cleansed the region of Croats four years before. Few would disagree with Croatian Prime Minister Ivo Sanader: the Krajina campaign of 1995 was "a brilliant, historic, military and police operation that we can be proud of."[3] It is simply difficult to imagine Croatia today without the success of Operation Storm.

At the same time, Croatia came to realize that entry into the EU (a much-desired privilege its neighbor Slovenia has already achieved) depended on Gotovina's capture – finally achieved in a Canary Islands restaurant in November 2005. Or rather: upon Croatia's willingness to see its shining moment, a victory that seemed at the time to redeem the nation from the guilt of Bosnia's destruction and the shame of Serb occupation, as itself flawed. Operation Storm saved Croatia, but it also helped to achieve President Tudjman's dream of a Croatia rid of its minorities. The price for independence, then, must still be paid.

No nation today is exempt from the obligation to pay its dues. Ramush Haradinaj was chosen in November 2004, at the age of thirty-six, as the Prime Minister of Kosovo. Five years earlier, he had been a commander in the KLA insurgency against Serb control. Another heroic moment of resistance to a regime accused of genocide – and it too was tainted. The ICTY, which began investigating Haradinaj before he became prime minister, charged him barely four months after his appointment with having supervised the killing both of Serb villagers and of Albanians accused of collaboration with the Serbs, in 1998–99. Haradinaj's decision to resign immediately and leave for The Hague has been seen as an important step forward for Kosovo; it is hard not to see a connection to Kosovo's progress toward independence over the course of 2005. It is true that Haradinaj's move – hardly surprising, considering NATO's continued presence in Kosovo – smacks of mere pragmatism, following rules set by powerful benefactors. However, the practice of submission to a court (or the judgment of history, for that matter), and acceptance of its verdict has real consequences, too.

The first UN commission on war crimes in Yugoslavia was created in the wake of revelations about the concentration camps of Serb-controlled Bosnia, in the summer of 1992; the ICTY did not take shape until 1994, when South African judge Richard Goldstone became prosecutor. Gary Bass shows, in his history of the tribunal, that the UN bureaucracy and most Western politicians hoped that little would come of the tribunal; it was, he writes, "evidently intended by many countries to be just another kind of reprimand, not an actual court with defendants in the dock."[4] That it grew to something with the power to affect countries' future, a place where prime ministers and generals might be tried, is thanks largely to its first two prosecutors, Goldstone and (from early 1996) Canadian Louise Arbour.

Since then, the tribunal has indicted 161 individuals for war crimes in Croatia, Bosnia, Kosovo, and Macedonia. Nearly all (with the great exceptions being General Ratko Mladić, commander at Srebrenica; and Bosnian Serb leader Radovan Karadzić) have been found, and subject to some level of legal action. To date, about one-third have been convicted; jail sentences have ranged from three years to life. The ICTY has become a model of how war crimes can be tried, inspiring similar efforts to prosecute those responsible for atrocities in Rwanda and Sudan.

So far the trials of those accused of war crimes appear to be the best approach to the truth. The trial of the ICTY's most famous prisoner, Slobodan Milošević, highlights the dangers of this pursuit of justice. Milošević, deported to The Hague shortly after losing power in October 2000, began his trial in February 2002; it continued until his sudden death in March 2006. He was charged with crimes against humanity and war crimes in Kosovo, Croatia, and Bosnia, and with genocide in Bosnia. From the beginning, he denied the tribunal's legitimacy, and used every opportunity to denounce the proceedings. His cross-examination of witnesses – he has refused a lawyer – allowed him to confront directly those who believed him responsible for the genocide they had survived – as if an Auschwitz survivor were subjected to questioning by Hermann Göring at Nuremberg. Playing to the audience back home, he sought to make one main point: that the entire proceedings were part of the West's efforts to make of Serbia an obedient colony, with Bosnians and Kosovars as willing accomplices. The ICTY in effect gave Milošević a bullhorn, gambling that truth would not only prevail in court, but could also calm, rather than inflame, passions in Serbia. In the end, a commitment to truth can not be imposed by a court; it remains impossible to tell where the boundary between pragmatism and genuine remorse lies.

Layer two: uncertain births

Doubts about the state's foundations are not confined to the former Yugoslavia, nor even to countries born in violence. After all, revolutionary change, of the kind that brought the end of communism in 1989, and then brought several nations their independence, is expected to be violent. Yet the revolutions of 1989 are notable precisely for their lack of bloodshed, as communist elites negotiated away their power with their opponents. What is the right way to have gained one's freedom? This may seem an odd or even superfluous question; for many East Europeans, it is a fundamental question about the legitimacy of the current state.

The countries most secure in their narratives of freedom are those who broke away with just a little violence. In the center of Riga, a small museum re-creates the atmosphere of the week in January 1991 when Latvian and Russian citizens together waited for Soviet troops to attack, in the wake of the deadly clash in Vilnius. There is even a scale model of the barricades, with artifacts from that long-ago vigil. On January 20, Soviet paramilitary units attacked the Ministry of Interior, killing five defenders and wounding a dozen more. While the museum is today nearly deserted, the legend of the barricades is still strong – as it is in Estonia, Lithuania, and Slovenia, too.

There is, perhaps surprisingly, less to celebrate and commemorate in the countries in between the Baltics and the Balkans. Neither the Poles nor the Hungarians – nor even the Czechs – celebrate an anniversary of communism's fall. This may be because the West remembers the fall of communism quite differently, through images of the opening of the Berlin Wall. That event, after all, came when the old regimes had already fallen in most of the region, and is in any case of limited symbolic meaning for most.

The Poles have long been obsessed with anniversaries. In the late nineteenth century, centenaries of the Polish Constitution (and of other last moments of glory before imperial neighbors dismantled the country) were important mobilizations on the way to regained independence. Today, the Polish calendar is full of remembered uprisings, victories, and defeats. Neither April 5, when the round table concluded, nor June 4, when the first elections were held, are on that list. In 1999, at the tenth anniversary of the round table, the main participants found they could only celebrate far away from home, at an academic conference in Ann Arbor, Michigan. That autumn, in Prague, the official atmosphere was more festive: Václav Havel welcomed world leaders of 1989 (Gorbachev, Bush, Kohl, Thatcher, Wałęsa) to the presidential palace for a symposium. But the mood was different on the streets, where graffiti proclaimed that "November 17 was treason," and on television, which aired a dramatization of a popular account of the events of 1989, claiming that it had all been a secret police set-up. In Hungary, meanwhile, Prime Minister Viktor Orbán attempted to bring an end to the "consensual politics" ushered in by the "Handshake Transition" of 1989.[5]

Considering that these societies were turning their backs on recent history just as they joined NATO, and as negotiations with the European Union began to accelerate, the ambivalence about the agreements that had made those successes possible was peculiar, to say the least. But it stemmed from a fear that too much had been bargained away. In Poland, the talk was of the "secret deals" that had suppposedly been struck with the communists, at a government compound called Magdalenka, to which top negotiators would repair whenever the round table threatened to come unglued. There, so the argument went, oppposition leaders agreed to allow the communists to control industry (through the nomenklaturization described in Chapter 1), in exchange for relinquishing political control.

The argument is somewhat different in Hungary, because those who negotiated with the regime were mostly from the conservative-nationalist opposition, while the left tended to hold the communists at arms' length. But Orbán was elected prime minister (in 1998) in part because he appeared to promise a fresh start, unburdened by communist skeletons or dissident litmus tests (though Orbán too had once been active in the anti-communist opposition). Not quite thirty-five years old when he took office, Orbán represented a search for innocence at the top; youthfulness, that is, was a way to negate the recent past. Nearly every country in the region has elected at least one thirty-something (or even a twenty-something) prime minister. It is easier, perhaps, to jettison the past than to confront it. One result has been, though, to leave them without a story of birth. As we will see in the last chapter, the entry into the European Union has perhaps filled that need for a fresh, unambiguous beginning.

One casualty of this distaste for 1989 is that the most visible heroes of that time, the anti-communist dissidents, largely disappeared from view within a few years. Only a very few politicians – such as Gábor Demszky, the popular and charismatic Mayor of Budapest, or Jacek Kuroń, until his death one of the most popular figures in Polish politics – could still, a decade or more after their initial victory, draw upon their dissident past as a source of political legitimacy. The decline of Havel is the most dramatic example. In January 1990, he was the obvious choice for President of Czechoslovakia. Ten years later, surveys showed him to have lost most of his popularity. In February 1999, nearly half of Czechs polled said he should resign.[6]

Why has this been the case? One popular theory is that former dissidents are a reproach to those who did not stand up against the communist regime. President Havel, indeed, often admonished his fellow citizens to acknowledge their complicity in the communist system. The general guilty conscience of collaboration, then, isolated him, and other dissident-heroes, too. A better explanation, though, would consider whether dissidents could adapt to the democratic politics they helped to secure. Those who succeeded, like Kuroń and Demszky, are usually men or women of action, trying incessantly to get concrete results of the most ordinary kind. Those who have failed are more likely contemplative figures, like Havel or Polish Prime Minister Tadeusz Mazowiecki, seemingly detached from the political fray, and thus unable to offer concrete solutions to their constituencies. Still other active figures, like Lech Wałęsa, sought to capitalize more on their laudable past than on the future, and found that approach ineffective after the first two or three years.

Layer three: the communist mirror

This is not to say that East Europeans have turned away from the communist past. Far from it: With some regularity, scandals about communist collaboration have erupted across the region throughout the post-communist period. From the beginning, East Europeans have asked themselves: was the communist regime that we endured illegitimate, or even evil? And if it was, whose fault was it? What constituted a crime, and what should be the punishment? At one extreme, there have been those who compare communist rule to that of Hitler or Stalin, and have called for Nuremberg-like trials; in Romania, this wish for terrible justice was granted a bit prematurely when a military tribunal ordered the summary execution of Nicolae and Elena Ceauşescu on December 25, 1989. The return of post-communist parties to power throughout Eastern Europe, however, suggests that such a cathartic break – which should, as at Nuremberg, imply that all who joined the party were implicated in a criminal organization – would have been impossible, and extravagant. "We cannot lay all the blame on those who ruled us before," Havel told his country in his New Year's Day address of 1990, "not only because this would not be true but also because it could detract from the responsibility each of us now faces – the responsibility to act on our own initiative."[7] Havel's position could imply that all are guilty – or that none is. No matter how normal, even benign, communist rule came to seem, the latter option is as unsatisfactory as the former.

The imperfect solution, taking the place of impossible trials, is *lustration* – the examination of the past (with the potential imposition of penalties) of those who choose to remain in public life. Presumably, people with hidden pasts could take advantage of the new democratic system to remain near the levers of power, and might cause trouble.

Others, intending to do good, might be blackmailed by someone who knew their past. These are the arguments in favor of lustration. The term was coined in Czechoslovakia, the first East European country to undertake a full review. The instigation, and the end of the post-revolutionary honeymoon, was the August 1991 coup in the Soviet Union. Suddenly, fears of the communists' return seemed quite real, and the earlier conciliation toward the communists and the secret police now appeared naive.

The Czechoslovak law on lustration affected thousands of high government positions: members of Parliament, officials in ministries and in the state-run media, police and military officers, even directors of state-owned companies. Anyone found to have collaborated with the State Security police, or who had certain positions in the Communist Party – names were checked against a registry in the Ministry of Interior – would be banned from public work for five years.

Lustration appeared to solve many problems, but it also raised new questions. The chief one is the source: lustration requires that one trust the files created by the secret police. The communist system, though, had thrived on lies both public and private; why would secret police officers *not* fabricate informers to impress their superiors? Second, were informers (many of whom had been painfully coerced into cooperating) really worse than, say, party officials who had then profited so well from the system, and who now lived on grand pensions, out of reach of lustration? And third, was not the essence of life under communism a kind of collaboration – of going along to get along, and tolerating an odious system? How could some kinds of collaboration be punished, and others not? Tina Rosenberg notes that Jiří Ruml, the head of the November 17 Commission charged in 1991 with lustrating members of Parliament, had in the early 1950s broadcast reports on show trials – yet this worthy contribution to communist repression did not make him vulnerable to lustration.[8]

All of this might be true – and Václav Havel made these points eloquently – but there was also a great need for clarity, some sense that the new was better than the old. The result, however, has been anything but clarity. Consider the case of Jan Kavan, who was named

Foreign Minister in 1998. He had fled the country in 1969, a student radical whose future was dim after the Soviet invasion that ended the Prague Spring. In London, he became one of the most active émigré organizers and publishers; he even snuck back into Czechoslovakia, and into other communist countries, over the years to improve contact between dissident circles and the West. In June 1990, he was elected to Parliament on the Civic Forum's slate. Yet nine months later, the November 17 Commission exposed him as having been a secret-police collaborator in London, who had informed his handler in the Czechoslovak Embassy about his émigré and British contacts, and had worked to undermine demonstrations protesting Czechoslovak crackdowns.[9]

The files were real; so were Kavan's conversations in London. So was the fact that Kavan was a difficult, sometimes irascible figure whose left-wing politics did not sit well with many of his closest colleagues. In the end, the question of whether or not he had knowingly become a collaborator was not nearly as important as a more contemporary one: Why did it matter? One reason, again, is a perverse resentment of dissidents, for having shown that opposition was possible. While Havel for a time rose above this, he too eventually endured the contempt of much of the Czech public, as well as accusations of collaboration. Second, lustration allowed post-communist society to purify its communist past. Communism had forced nearly everyone to give in to small or large compromises to keep one's job, one's family, one's aspirations. Lustration promised to make things black and white, to identify the villains so that everyone else could be absolved of collaboration. At the same time, it affirmed the devious power of the communist state, retrospectively justifying people's decisions not to stand up and resist; since even resistance was tainted, it was also futile. And third, lustration offered the hope that the new order would be unlike the old one: it would be morally upright and free of the evil that was communism. That quest for purity, even at the expense of truth, however, was not unlike that of the Stalinists, who coaxed purge victims into confession for the good of the party, even if "objectively" they had committed no crime.[10]

The Poles tried a rather different approach, veering all over the map in an attempt to avoid the mistakes of the Czechs. Accepting his post in August 1989, Prime Minister Tadeusz Mazowiecki asked his nation to "draw a thick line" between the present and the past. He meant that his government should be judged only on its deeds, and not on the burdens it inherited, yet the "thick line" has come to symbolize a supposed absolution granted to communist leaders. An early attempt to compile a list of collaborators (like the one in Prague, which was leaked to the press in 1992) brought down a Solidarity-led government. In early 1992, newly-chosen Minister of Interior and former dissident Antoni Macierewicz announced he was prepared to release the names of all collaborators if directed by Parliament; when such a law (regarding only prominent public officials) was passed, he turned over a list, which was promptly leaked – on June 4, the third anniversary of Polish communism's fall. Unlike in Czechoslovakia, there was no attempt to review the names, which included President Wałęsa (code name: Bolek). Years later, it would be proven that many of the relevant documents were simply fabrications of ambitious policemen. The list came quickly to be seen as a political ploy, and the Parliament that same day voted no confidence in the government.

While, for some, such lists to this day are proof of the corruption of the entire political establishment, others have learned the lesson of care. Lustration in any case stalled in Poland, as a post-communist government, elected in 1993, dragged its feet. To former communists, lustration was an "exorcism of the past,"[11] and many people seemed to agree. Wałęsa himself lost the election of 1995 to a former communist, in part because his focus on his opponent's past wearied voters. Not until 1999 was a lustration law passed; significantly, it punished not membership, nor even collaboration, but lying about it: those government officials or judges who admitted to collaboration were named in the government gazette, but could continue to work, or run for office. Only those whose declarations were found to be untruthful were banned from high office. More than a few admitted collaborators have won election: depending on one's perspective, this was either evidence of Polish voters' gullibility, or of their mature focus on candidates' accomplishments and skills, rather than on the past.

One factor that has influenced growing public indifference to lustration is the fact that often (though not as a rule) high-profile col-laborators have turned out to be right-wing, nationalist politicians. For example, when the right-wing party Fidesz lost the 2002 parlia-mentary election in Hungary, it retaliated by exposing prime min-ister-designate Péter Medgyessy of the Hungarian Socialist Party as a collaborator. Medgyessy admitted his work in counterintelligence, and kept his job; the ensuing hunt through the secret-police files, however, revealed that several ministers in the Fidesz government, including Finance Minister Zsigmond Járai, had also collaborated in one form or another. Thus, past collaboration reveals nothing about later political positions, except to the most conspiracy-minded observer. And as the Medgyessy case shows, admissions of collabora-tion by former communists usually carry with them no penalty, as most voters have no illusions about them, anyway. The result has been a marked decline in interest in lustration or in secret-police files. The lustration controversies have simply shown (in less abstract terms) what Havel suggested in 1990: if everyone was at some level a collaborator, then all that matters is one's work today.

There are two areas in which putting the past on trial does still matter. First, nearly every country that existed prior to 1989 has attempted to try its communist leaders. With the notable excep-tions of Romania's execution of Ceaușescu, and Serbia's export of Milošević to The Hague, there has been little success. Todor Zhivkov – who ruled communist Bulgaria for thirty-five years, far longer even than Stalin ruled the Soviet Union – was the first to face charges. In 1990, a commission created by Parliament charged Zhivkov with embezzling state funds and abuse of power – in particular, the in-citing of ethnic hatred through his 1984 campaign to "Bulgarize" ethnic Turks – and summoned him to account for his rule before the people of Bulgaria. A year later, his trial on embezzlement (the ethnic hatred charge was dropped) began. The charge was a resonant one: as were Romanians who gazed upon the Ceaușescus' palaces (now preserved as tourist attractions), Bulgarians were both fascinated and repulsed by stories of the Zhivkovs' wealth. The trial stretched until September 1992, when Zhivkov, by then eighty-one years old, was sentenced to seven years of house arrest. He served most of his sentence before it was overturned in 1997, just a year before his death. By then, as will be discussed below, nostalgia had triumphed over revenge as the dominant emotion felt toward communist leaders.

Zhivkov, though, had ruled during long periods of stability; rather less fortunate were those leaders associated primarily with the unstable last years of communism. Just a few months after defeating him in the 1992 election, Albania's president Sali Berisha placed Ramiz Alia, head of state for the previous seven years, on trial (along with nine co-defendants) for "misappropriation of state property and [for] violating the rights and freedoms of Albanian citizens."[12] In this way, the new government could draw a contrast with communist rule. In the dock, Alia obliged by warmly praising the communist era and its founder, Enver Hoxha. He received a sentence of nine years. That same year, Berisha (who had himself, not so long before, been a Communist Party dignitary) had his main rival, Socialist Party Chair Fatos Nano, imprisoned; four years later, Nano acceded to power and returned the favor by having several members of Berisha's cabinet arrested. Thus, Albania's leaders used the courtroom to advocate rival versions of the past: who was the democratizer, and who stood in democracy's way? With authoritarian rule never that far from the surface during the 1990s, the questions about communism's return were quite real.

The longest-running effort to prosecute a communist leader, however, has been in Poland. Almost continuously since he stepped down as president in 1990, General Wojciech Jaruzelski has been on trial. Unlike his peers elsewhere, the ascetic Jaruzelski has been charged not with economic crimes, but for his role in the massacre of shipyard workers in Gdansk in 1970; the imposition of martial law in December 1981; and the massacre of strikers at the Wujek mine that same month. The trials and hearings, before Parliament or in civilian courts, have stopped and started numerous times over the years, through illnesses (of Jaruzelski and other defendants), procedural conflicts, and appeals. It is as if, wishing to avoid an unpleasant decision – since to acquit raises the question of whether anyone can be held responsible for these specific tragedies, while conviction of a man who reached agreement with Solidarity in 1989 and then voluntarily resigned his presidency in 1990 might seem untoward – the Polish courts have instead placed Jaruzelski in purgatory, forcing him to testify constantly until death.

In contrast to his Balkan co-defendants, Jaruzelski represents not communism's golden age of stability; nor does he defiantly endorse its repressive past. Instead, his challenge is more subtle: Jaruzelski presents himself as a Polish patriot, bound by the duty and honor of a soldier to defend his country. To many in Poland, martial law was an unfortunate necessity; the image of a nation divided cannot be erased by judicial means. And so almost by default, Poland has devised another exploration of the gray zone of communist uncertainty. Was communist Poland the "jolliest barrack in the Soviet camp," where dissidents lived in comparative freedom, or a brutal regime of prisons, censors, and deprivation? The latter seemed correct in 1990, but gradually Polish politicians began to see another side. The Solidarity activist Zbigniew Bujak tells of being invited to address trade union members in Guatemala in the mid-1990s. When he punctuated his tale of martial law by remarking that at least 150 people had died, there was an awkward silence; afterward, his hosts politely explained that some 150,000 had died in their struggle. It was difficult, after such an encounter, to see Poland as a concentration camp, or Jaruzelski as its sadistic guard.

Yet the younger generation, to whom the difficult choices of communism were just an abstraction, found such gray answers hard to accept. What good were halfway measures and balanced assessments, if communism, so it turned out, had to fall anyway? In early 1990, Alexander Dubček was interviewed by a young reporter. Dubček, the leader of Czechoslovakia in the Prague Spring, still considered himself a socialist. He had been banished by the Husák regime to work in the forestry department in a distant Slovak province. In 1989, he had been welcomed by enthusiastic crowds on Prague's Wenceslas Square. Though the presidency eluded him, he was chosen Speaker of the lower chamber of the legislature; he was one of the most recognized faces in Czechoslovakia. Yet the reporter Jaroslav Hanzel tore into him:

> JH: Because of your mistakes – your silence both during the invasion and afterwards – people have come to feel that the tragedy

of 1968 is directly linked to your character, and particularly your
"softness."

AD: What softness? Even now there are all sorts of things that emotion keeps me from saying. When the intervention took place,
I didn't give up. Most of us completely rejected the occupation
without any hesitation whatsoever. At the same time, I had to
find the strength to join [Prime Minister] Černík and [President]
Svoboda in giving instructions that the advancing army of occupation not be opposed militarily.

JH: That's right! Yet again in the history of modern Czechoslovakia,
its people fail to put up any resistance! You're to blame more
than anyone else!

AD: Does the public blame me? I don't think so. Certain individuals
do. But they judge the past through the prism of the present.[13]

Layer four: Stalin's shadow

The Prague Spring – like Poland's martial law, or the Croatian
Spring of 1971, or the negotiations that ended communism in
many countries – were events that could not be agreed upon, precisely because they represented a middle way: non-violent reform of
communist dictatorship. The central problems of communism and
resistance will have to be considered anew by each generation. In
other matters, though, all could concur that some crimes were and
would be crimes. Still, there has been much room for interpretation,
and justice has proven elusive.

In most countries, the era of severe repressions ended in 1956.
Before then, arbitrary arrest, torture, and summary trials were common, though the scale never approached that of Stalin's Great Purge
in the USSR in the 1930s. After 1956, with the partial exceptions
of Albania and Romania, such repression became rarer, replaced
by the mundane, even petty tactics that yielded the moral ambiguities discussed earlier: the coerced collaboration, the denial of jobs
or of entrance to university, the confiscated passport. The earlier
period was much easier to prosecute, as the names of police, the
interrogators, the torturers, prosecutors, and judges were known.
But two problems have made even this reckoning with the past
quite difficult. First, what precisely was the crime? And second,

how meaningful were prosecutions of forty-year-old crimes? In most cases, the accused were elderly. While prosecutions of Holocaust perpetrators established a precedent for this, there were no criminals of comparable stature still alive in Eastern Europe. While conscience, and popular outrage, demanded that those responsible for Stalinist crimes be held accountable, this has proven almost impossible. Consider the case of Helena Wolińska Brus. In 1950, she was a military prosecutor, signing warrants for the arrest of many Poles who had fought in the anti-Nazi underground during World War Two. Many of those arrested received the death penalty. One of those arrested, Władysław Bartoszewski (in the late 1990s, Poland's Minister of Foreign Affairs), recalled being shown a sheaf of blank warrants that Wolińska had signed. Yet by the time Polish prosecutors caught up with her, she was nearly eighty, the wife of an Oxford professor.[14] She has refused to return, and has charged that the case is motivated by antisemitism. Justice may be clear in such a case, but achieving anything beyond a Pyrrhic victory seems unlikely.

The Stalinist era has thus become a focus of commemoration instead. A day in Budapest can reveal the divergent ways in which one can recall the crimes of Stalinism. On Andrassy Street, once and now again one of the most elegant avenues on the Pest side, stands the House of Terror, housed in an grand fin-de-siècle edifice, once the headquarters of the Hungarian Security Police (and before that, the fascist Arrow Cross movement). The *Terror Háza* was the creation of Prime Minister Viktor Orbán and his advisor on matters of Hungarian history, Mária Schmidt, now the museum's director; it opened in 2002. The outside of the building is framed by a steel wall, jutting out across the sidewalk four stories high, then forming an awning at the roofline; the word "Terror," cut into the steel, casts a shadow on the sidewalk below. Inside, the exhibits are grim reminders of Hungary's suffering in the years from communist takeover through the aftermath of the revolution of 1956. In the basement, one can view the cells where victims were tortured. Yet amidst the sobering pictures of prisons and camps, and their inmates and guards, one gradually notices two things: First, this general portrayal of Stalinist terror almost completely neglects the preceding decade of terror, under native authoritarian and fascist leaders; second, the rows of portraits of "victimizers" subtly connect, for the Hungarian viewer, with contemporary right-wing rhetoric claiming that the perpetrators of communist terror were not themselves Hungarian, but Jewish. The museum is thus an argument about the nature of the Hungarian nation, and also a political argument: terror, and danger, comes from the left. The visitor who wishes simply to remember and to learn is reminded that this is a museum of present conflicts, too.

The opposite approach – one that, while more enjoyable, is also disturbing in its own way – can be found in the Szoborpark, located at the southern edge of the city on the Buda side. Here have been gathered most of the statues erected in communist Budapest, which, after 1989, became ripe for discarding. The statue park opened in 1993, defying those who had called for the statues to be destroyed. Forty-one Marxes, Lenins, Soviet soldiers, Hungarian worker militias, and so on line the paths. These statues do not inspire solemnity, but one does not feel like laughing, either. Instead, there is only irony. The guidebook informs us that we are tracing figure eights, "the mathematical symbol for infinity. Whatever adventures you may have on your route, you will always return to the 'true path.'"[15] A brick wall at the end of the park apparently symbolizes the "dead end" of communism, forcing visitors to return to the entrance and the gift shop, where (in 1996) one could purchase a small can labeled "the last breath of socialism" or a cassette tape with songs and speeches from the Stalinist era. One must take the architect at his word: this is not meant to be a joke. But while its purpose is surely to underscore the ambiguity of the communist experience, unlike the black-and-white, forbidding *Terror Háza*, that ambiguity is simply neutral. The Statue Park becomes a pleasant diversion, as well as a place of exile for unwanted images. One museum gives communism a post-modern veil, while the other places it in the center, overwhelming even the Holocaust.

It may be inevitable that contemporary politics is fought in part on the terrain of the past, in countries whose recent history has offered so many opportunities to be victim, resister, collaborator, or oppressor. For this reason, states are reluctant to let history out of their hands – as happened, for example, in South Africa, where the Truth and Reconciliation Commission led by Bishop Desmond Tutu remained entirely independent. There has been no Truth and Reconciliation Commission in Eastern Europe (though the idea has surfaced). That space has been taken, instead, by independent movements of historians and archivists, seeking simply to document what came before. An inspiration for such groups is Memorial, founded by dissidents in Moscow in 1987 to document Stalinist repression in the Soviet Union. Similar institutes operate across the region. Though direct or indirect state funding nearly always provides crucial support (and biases of different sorts naturally have not disappeared), the production of history has for the most part passed from government to historians both professional and amateur.

Layer five: dark passage

As the House of Terror in Budapest shows us, the hardest task for all East European societies is to move back beyond 1945, to understand how World War Two both made today's nations, and left them with troubling, unexplored legacies. A peek into the dungeons of the Holocaust and Nazi occupation makes the communist era seem quite simple in contrast.

The nations of today's Eastern Europe fall into three categories: those that were active allies of the Nazis; those that became nominally independent puppet states of Hitler's Germany; and those that were occupied. Those in the first category – primarily Hungary and Romania – face the simplest task, for their complicity has never been in doubt. Still, that same native fascism can be and has been twisted around to serve as a source of national pride. A good example of this is the veneration of Romanian dictator Ion Antonescu, who ruled from 1940 to 1944. Marshal Antonescu was for a time allied with the fascist Iron Guard, before destroying them and claiming to rule above any party. Desiring to recover territory annexed by the Soviet Union in 1940, he joined the German attack in 1941; he was executed after a brief trial in 1946. Viewed one way, then, he was responsible for much of Romania's misfortune during the war and after, including the destruction of Romania's Jewish and Roma communities. But his drive to reunite Romanian lands; his alliance with a strong Western power, and of course his execution at Soviet hands have all made him seem, to some, an inspiration for Romania's post-communist future. Nor were these the fantasies of a few old men. During the first election campaign, in May 1990, a pro-government newspaper printed excerpts from a letter Antonescu wrote chiding opposition parties for obstructionism; the parallel to the present was clear enough.[16] Ironically, as the man who both crushed a fascist rebellion and was himself ousted by a king (Michael, the same man who sought to return to the throne in 1990), Antonescu even seemed a figure suitable for modern politics. Not until 2001, when the unveiling of a bust of Antonescu in Bucharest appeared to threaten Romania's NATO aspirations, did veneration of the wartime leader become politically unacceptable.[17]

The war experience was even more treacherous for the puppet states. Neither Croatia nor Slovakia had any other period of independence, in over 700 years, to point to besides the Nazi protectorates; to deny those regimes would seem to call into question the new states' right to exist. Thus Franjo Tudjman, as noted previously, revived the symbols of Ante Pavelić's Independent State of Croatia (1941–45) – though not, except obliquely, the memory of Pavelić himself. In Slovakia, Monsignor Jozef Tiso is inextricably tied to the state of which he was president from its beginning in 1939, and himself embodies the ambiguities of that state: proud keeper of the flame of Slovak consciousness, but also responsible for the deportation of Slovak Jews. Tiso's name was often invoked by Slovaks advocating independence in 1990–92; they gained a key ally when popular politician Vladimír Mečiar adopted their language and cause in early 1991.[18] Tiso's supporters have articulated a yet higher aim: beatification by the Catholic Church. Tiso, they argue, was a martyr of communism, and a priest who fought for virtue amid evil. Perhaps, even, he is like Slovakia in its quest for independence and purity. But in Slovakia, too, the prospect of NATO and EU membership dampened enthusiasm for the wartime state.

There are few moments in international or interethnic relations of post-communist East European history that do not evoke World War Two. Russian requests for transit of goods and people across Lithuania or Poland recall Nazi demands for a corridor; Western attempts to deal with Slobodan Milošević echo the appeasement of Hitler at

Munich, 1938. The most difficult reminders, though, are the ones that are no longer there. Denial of domestic complicity in the Holocaust was almost universal across the region in the first post-communist years. Croatia elected as its first president a historian: Tudjman had been a proponent of the thesis that Pavelić's regime had not killed 600,000 Serbs and Jews at Jasenovac (the largest concentration camp not under Nazi control), but at most 60,000 total; under Tudjman, the camp site, which had been an obligatory pilgrimage goal under Tito, was allowed to fall into disrepair. Visiting the camp in June 1996, Tudjman sought to recast it as a symbol not of Croatian murder of ethnic minorities, but of common suffering, including Croatian nationalists murdered in the communist era. Having just the previous year expelled most of Croatia's Serbs, Tudjman was attempting to provide his people with a cleansed past, too.

In both Romania and Hungary (the latter, too, presided over by a historian, József Antall, in the years 1990–93), the Holocaust has been an uncomfortable story. Antisemitic nationalism, as we saw in the previous chapter, has had a powerful effect on national politics in both countries. As in Slovakia, it is difficult to separate the country's struggle for freedom from its persecution of Jews. Nowhere has modern confrontation with the Holocaust been more dramatic than in Poland. In early 2000, American scholar Jan Gross published a book documenting the murder by the Poles of the town of Jedwabne of virtually all their Jewish neighbors, on one day in July 1941.[19] Predictably, a storm of denial greeted the book. Yet what has been surprising is that the public has generally come to accept Gross's version of events. When President Aleksander Kwaśniewski apologized on behalf of all Poles for the crime, during sixtieth-anniversary ceremonies in Jedwabne, nearly half of Poles surveyed supported the apology. Given that Polish national consciousness includes the strong belief that the Nazis viewed Poles as next in line for extermination after the Jews, the strong support for teaching schoolchildren that Poles were murderers as well as victims is remarkable.[20]

Making it right

What brings about success in dealing with the past? The easy answer would have something to do with Western pressure, with democratic traditions, and maybe also the penetration of Western-generated norms of human rights into civic culture. The examples of changes of heart in Romania or Croatia, above, would seem to support this argument. If this were the case, however, few countries would be more open to rethinking the past than the Czech Republic: where a renowned moral philosopher was president for thirteen years; where democracy thrived before communism; and where Western presence is unsurpassed in the region. Yet even in the face of clear benefits of openness, Czechs have resisted examination of the most shameful episode in their history: the killing of thousands of Czech Germans during forced expulsions in 1945–46. In a 2002 poll, just 3 percent responded that an apology was appropriate – and this a dozen years after Havel's first statement of apology. In Poland, a comparable (earlier) survey found about one-third supporting an apology – though Polish expulsions were far milder, and their own suffering at German hands, far greater.[21]

There are two likely explanations. First, no country in Eastern Europe can feel more secure about its national identity than Poland. Size does matter in this case; fears of threats to language, or ethnicity simply have greater resonance in smaller countries, or those (like the Czech Republic) founded recently. Secondly, civil society: the roots of anti-communist resistance go far deeper in Poland than anywhere else. The Solidarity movement, as it developed over a decade above and below ground, proved an encounter with democracy; tolerance for, and even acceptance of, differing viewpoints was a common experience. In addition, Solidarity writers rethought Polish concepts of martyrdom, and reexamined Polish history, and especially Poles' relations with neighboring nations – to an extent not possible in countries where the underground press was vastly smaller. Western pressures for reconciliation, or calls for moral renewal, only compensate, in other countries, for the lack of one or both of these factors.

Recognition of the crimes of the past, however, has only raised new questions. How should wrongs be made right again? In most cases, the time for trials or other legal remedies is long past; indeed, in some cases (as in Jedwabne, or in the case of some Stalinists) the perpetrators were punished during the communist era. At the other end of the spectrum is memorialization. But as Tudjman demonstrated at Jasenovac, even an established memorial can be willfully misread. Apologies continue to play an important role; for example, in 2004 the leaders of Serbia and Croatia apologized to Bosnians for their countries' role in the genocide. How, though, can victims be compensated? In every country in Eastern Europe, communism began with expropriation: property passed from the "exploiters" to the state. Private homes became apartments or kindergartens, churches became movie theaters, bombed-out buildings gave way to new office towers, castles became state-run tourist traps. This process was made easier by the war: the communists were often taking from people who had left or been killed. Some property was expropriated twice, by the Nazis and communists. Forty-five years later, as privatization became universal practice, the state would obviously have to get rid of its holdings, especially if it wanted to encourage investment by proving to the West that property rights would be respected. And thus restitution – the return of confiscated goods or their equivalent – came to dominate evaluations of the past.

This restitution is fundamentally different from that familiar in Western jurisprudence, where a criminal pays some compensation to the crime victim. In post-communist Eastern Europe, states that were not themselves considered liable for the deeds of the previous regime none the less sought to rectify those misfortunes, at their own cost. (Separately, communist parties were made to surrender their vast real estate holdings.) There were, of course, many minefields in the restitution discussions; particularly treacherous was the problem of the time period to be covered. For example, Hungary's law on restitution, passed in 1991, promised compensation for property taken in 1949 and after. This covered only those harmed by the Stalinist regime; Jews who lost property during the war would not be helped. A year later, the cut-off point was moved back to 1939. To Hungarian nationalists, this had the effect of equating the communist and wartime regimes. On the other hand, the law's provision for only partial compensation (justified on the grounds that the state was not the culpable party, and in any event could not afford more) appeared to violate international treaties calling for Holocaust victims to receive full compensation.[22]

In the Czech Republic, compensation problems raised other

painful issues. A law passed in 1991 set the cut-off point as the communist coup of February 1948. Not only Jews dispropriated by the Nazis were affected; so, too, were the millions of Czech-German expellees. The prospect of giving huge swaths of Sudetenland cities back to Germans has made it politically infeasible to change the law (though ways have been found to extend compensation to Jews).

The problem, fundamentally – though in the end irrelevant to moral questions – is that Eastern Europe has changed so much in the last seventy years. The cities became everywhere dominated by the majority ethnic group – meaning that someone would lose a home, or a school, or a livelihood if property were returned. In places where the Catholic Church was particularly strong, even believers found themselves disturbed by the prospect of the Church suddenly becoming a major property owner again. Another victim of communist expropriation was the nobility; could castles, urban mansions, and huge landholdings really be returned to families who had fled sixty years ago? The intervening decades of modernization and industrialization – not to mention communist propaganda – made this unpalatable. Finally, what about émigrés in general? While the Czech Republic has excluded them from claiming compensation unless they regain citizenship, other countries such as Estonia have opened restitution to all. The result, in the latter case, was a staggering number of claims. Though restitution is considered necessary to economic credibility and growth, the enormity of the undertaking, and the amount of state property lost without compensation, has also taken its toll on economies. The issue is at heart a moral one, as Joan Lofgren writes about Estonia: "The way the property was seized or abandoned, usually connected to political repression, made [restitution] especially personal. Memories of a knock on the door in the night, or of fleeing before that knock came, never to return to home or farm, still provide stark images."[23] Though restitution appears to bring Eastern Europe back to a past it is not sure it wants, it turns out to be a key to leaving that past behind.

Ultimately, what is the aim of all this revisiting of the past? Only in some cases – such as the confiscation of party-held properties – do policies of addressing the past have an immediate practical goal. More generally, the objective is reconciliation, bringing a measure of peace to democratizing societies. The images of crowds of Serbs greeting returning Bosnian Muslims with sticks and stones is a reminder that restitution (or apology, or trials) does not in itself heal wounds. Still, broader acceptance of its necessity is both a sign and a cause of increased tolerance, both in domestic and international relations. Debates about history throughout the world have shown this to be true; the difference in Eastern Europe is that working through the past turns out to be a requirement for international standing.

The case for nostalgia

It sometimes seems, in discussion of the uses of history in contemporary Eastern Europe, as if observers are constantly scolding those societies for their attachment to the past; they imply a contrast with supposedly more modern societies that have put aside historical squabbles. But to ignore history is surely no better an approach to the present. In Tony Judt's apt phrasing, Eastern Europe may have "too much memory," but Western Europe has "a shortage of memory."[24] Interest in one's past is hardly a bad thing. That is so when we speak of the more distant past – essential to national consciousness, and thus the sense of community that may strengthen a society – but also when we think of the more recent past.

At least since the communist parties first began to return to power in 1993–94 (see next chapter), nostalgia for the communist past has both baffled and alarmed foreign and domestic proponents of the post-communist order. Josip Tito has his own website (www.titoville.com) where he shares his favorite photos and offers words of wisdom from beyond the grave to adoring Yugoslavs. Several towns in Poland have recently erected statues of or named streets after Edward Gierek, leader from 1971 to 1980. In many countries, 1970s television dramas in which imperialist spies are unmasked (presumably on their way to humiliating show trials and prison) have enjoyed new popularity. And all this is not to mention the return of communist leaders, or the large numbers of people who profess a preference for the communist era.

For what, really, are people nostalgic? When Warsaw's Zachęta Gallery staged an exhibit re-creating a slice of the 1960s in 2000, complete with a threadbare café and surly cashier, it was a sensation. But were visitors longing for the cruelty and the shortages, or perhaps willfully ignoring the bad in desperate pursuit of a simpler time? Not exactly, writes Peeter Sauter, recalling warmly his youth in Soviet Estonia: "A longing for certain things is not a longing for life under communism, but rather for what was then desired so intensely. In other words, for what was then forbidden."[25] The deep satisfaction from acquiring scarce goods, or being the first to hear a Western rock band, or catching Radio Free Europe on the shortwave late at night: these emotions, and not the life itself, are the subject of nostalgia. Sauter is undoubtedly right. True, there are some who long for Ceauşescu, Tiso, or even Stalin out of a desire to see their country powerful, and rid of its problems. But for most, nostalgia is not the product of failure, but rather of maturity. One can add that the communist past today offers something for nearly everyone. For some, it represents stability and relative prosperity: a time when one could afford necessities now increasingly out of reach. For others, communist regimes could boast greater attention to social issues, ranging from abortion to homelessness, than its successors. For others still, it represents a time of national greatness. And for those under thirty, it is but an exotic land, represented now by the posters in retro-communist cafés in many a city.

History is not simply a set of facts to be mastered, but a way of understanding the past; multiple pasts, while frustrating to the historian, are also themselves an approximation of democracy. The wonder is not that East Europeans have multiple pasts: that every event or phenomenon of the past, from the Holocaust to police informers to vintage automobiles, have different meanings for different people. The surprise is that the mutability of memory is becoming accepted. As even admitted informers like Péter Medgyessy are elected to office, or Poles determine that an apology is owed whether or not Germans were also present in Jedwabne during the massacre, or former Yugoslavs recognize that sometimes, there is something of their disappeared country worth remembering – was it any wonder that the main bridge in Bosnian Mostar was still, in 1995, named after Marshal Tito? – they weave a fabric of tolerance that underlies the progress made since 1989. Rather than leaving the past behind, Eastern Europe must carry it along into the future.

4 | Portraits of hubris: democratic politics

On New Year's Day, 1990, Václav Havel stepped on to a balcony in the presidential castle to address the crowd gathered to cheer his inauguration. He depicted the previous regime as aloof, and ignorant of the everyday lives of the citizens, and congratulated his fellow Czechs and Slovaks on the "enormous strength" they had shown in overturning communism so suddenly and peacefully the previous autumn. Havel promised that policies would be based upon morality, recalling the ideals of Czechoslovakia's first democracy under President Masaryk.

> Politics ought to be a reflection of the aspiration to contribute to
> the happiness of the community and not of the need to deceive or
> pillage the community ... Politics does not have to be the art of the
> possible, especially if this means the art of speculating, calculating,
> intrigues, secret agreements, and pragmatic maneuvering, but ... it
> can also be the art of the impossible, that is the art of making both
> ourselves and the world better.

His rousing finale paraphrased Masaryk: "People," he proclaimed, "your country has returned to you."[1]

Havel captured all the optimism of that revolutionary moment in that one line. Note, however, how much faith he places in the workings of politics: The country became the people's because it had a new president. Indeed, it seemed then that political change alone would make happiness attainable. This perspective owes much to previous revolutions, in which political change, grounded in ideology, appeared to be fundamental. The revolutions of 1989 were not, in contrast, guided by one political elite. Instead, they offered the possibility of varied, even contradictory political solutions. Yet that variety is sometimes overlooked: the apparent lack of a "Third Way" makes it easy to assume that there is but one trajectory.

Throughout the post-communist era, political change has not only been the most noticeable, but also the most easily measured. Each year, for example, Freedom House rates countries' level of democracy on a scale of 1 to 7, considering the freedom of elections, the independence of the media, the rule of law, etc. In 1989, all except "partly free" (thanks to reformist communism) Poland, Hungary, and Yugoslavia, ranked as "not free"; in 2005, Eastern European countries (with a few exceptions in the Western Balkans, namely Bosnia-Hercegovina, Macedonia, Albania, and Kosovo) have earned the "free" label.[2] These assessments, shaped as they are by American assumptions about democracy and capitalism, tell us as much about their authors as about their subjects, however. It is also true that, just as the creation of nation-states from multicultural empires leaves many minorities on the margins, so too democratic change (and the affirmation of property rights, a key measure for Freedom House) excludes many groups that may have felt less excluded before. Thus, political change may also be easier to understand if we approach it having already explored the economic, social, and cultural processes taking place simultaneously. Perhaps then the rapid march of elections, parties, and leaders will not just be a series of names and dates, but trends in a broader regional context.

To begin with, it is important to remember that free elections and democratic leaders do not in themselves add up to political liberty, unless society is able to take advantage of these things. Many populists of an authoritarian bent (and not only in Eastern Europe) have been elected in more-or-less-free votes, with a nominally free press, and against viable candidates. Therefore, while it is of course true that political developments shape the economy, society, and the culture, the opposite is also true, and will be emphasized here.

Change before democracy

Let us return to January 1990. Havel had actually been elected president not by the grateful citizens of Czechoslovakia, but by Parliament, in a unanimous vote. That Parliament, in turn, had begun its term in the communist regime; most of its members had been chosen by the Czechoslovak Communist Party as worthy, reliable comrades, and had run unopposed. The rest had been selected by the opposition, in the wake of the Velvet Revolution, as part of the negotiation that removed President Gustáv Husák from power; the worst toadies of the regime were excused from their parliamentary duties and replaced by opposition activists. This hybrid Parliament, with not a single popular mandate in the building, had raised its hands to approve Havel as president, and would govern until democratic elections were held in June.

The juxtaposition of a figure so patently democratic as Havel and a thoroughly undemocratic institution supporting him reminds us just how deep the roots of the old system were, and how long they would last. Indeed, historians do not write of the "post-tsarist" regime in Soviet Russia or "post-Nazi" Germany; "post-communist" means a period defined in part by the persistence of the communist political legacy. A look around the region on the day of Havel's address confirms this. Albania had not begun any sort of change; the Baltic republics had, but remained within the Soviet Union. That spring, all three Baltic republics would declare independence, but the world would largely ignore them until the USSR collapsed eighteen months later. The Yugoslavs were about to gather for a Party Congress that would sound the death knell for the country; so far, only Slovenes and Croats had founded independent political parties. Tanks still roamed Bucharest's streets in the chaotic throes of Ceaușescu's violent downfall in Romania, while in Bulgaria Zhivkov had fallen and been denounced but the communists still ruled – though they were about to begin negotiations with the opposition. Hungary was still under control of the Hungarian Socialist Party (it had dropped "Workers" from its title), and was preparing for its first elections. Only in Poland did a new, non-communist government rule, though communists controlled key ministries. The round table agreement there had carefully apportioned seats in Parliament between (old) regime and (soon to be ruling) opposition, and had assured that a communist would be chosen president. This was still a revolution: our snapshot captures countries in the midst of change to a new way of conducting business. It was a revolution, however, conducted with neither gun nor broom, but with non-violent persuasion.

The scope of this still-incomplete revolution was already apparent, and it seemed possible to some that democracy could be rethought from scratch – especially since forty-five years of communism had alienated society from political practice. The Helsinki Citizens' Assembly, an outgrowth of the networks of dissidents and their colleagues in Western Europe, was formed in Prague in October 1990 to promote civic activism from below, creating citizenship not through passports, but though active engagement across borders. Today, the Assembly has virtually disappeared from Eastern Europe (except for Tuzla, in Bosnia). The rapidity of change meant that societies everywhere chose familiar forms of participatory government.

Even so, there were difficult choices to make. A president chosen by Parliament might be less democratic, but – not having to campaign – would be less likely to be populist, too. A senate might seem an extravagance in a small country. Proportional representation or single-member districts each had their advantages. The most basic question, given the scale of change necessary, was whether democracy was even appropriate. Could one overhaul the economic system (shock therapy or no) while listening to the will of the people? Lech Wałęsa proposed in December 1989 that Parliament grant Prime Minister Tadeusz Mazowiecki special powers of decree to hasten economic transformation; he returned to the idea (now as president) in June 1991.[3] Both times, the government declined the offer, preferring democracy over efficiency.

The most powerful asset at the new governments' disposal was the honeymoon, the window of opportunity during which citizens were willing to tolerate painful change. The question, though, was just what was it that people expected to take place. How important, relative to one another, were freedom of speech and prosperity? Or dignity vs. freedom to travel? Uncertainty about popular desires was an additional reason for bringing about free elections as soon as possible.

The first free election was held in Hungary, in March–April 1990. A popular election poster contrasted a young couple kissing on a park bench with a slightly creepy kiss between two elderly communist leaders and the slogan "You choose." This was the first democratic test for a former communist party, and the result was clear: the socialists received less than 10 percent of the seats. The rightist Hungarian Democratic Forum (HDF) won handily, with half the votes in the second round, and formed a right-of-center coalition government headed by József Antall. Croatia and Slovenia held their elections the following month, laying the groundwork for independence the following year. Slovenes split their vote between a Parliament controlled by an anti-communist coalition, led by a Christian Democrat prime minister, and a reformist communist president, Milan Kučan. In Croatia, Franjo Tudjman and his HDZ dominated. In May, Romanians overwhelmingly voted for the National Salvation Front, in an election that, like Croatia's, epitomized concerns about whether East European societies really had a democratic choice. By this time, conflicts between opposition and the old ex-communists in the Front led many to assume the vote was rigged. International observers swore the vote was legitimate; the problem was rather the information voters brought with them to the ballot box. This first wave of elections concluded with the victory of the Socialist Party in Bulgaria and of the Civic Forum/Public without Violence coalition in Czechoslovakia, in June; Macedonia and Bosnia held their first elections in November, and Albania, last, the following spring.

These elections were really affirmations of change, plebiscites on the revolutions. Only in one case, Hungary, was there a major split within the anti-communist opposition; in the first round of voting, the HDF had narrowly edged out the post-dissident Alliance of Free Democrats. Everywhere else, voters either chose between the opposition forces or the post-communists, or were presented with a popular front (as in Romania) claiming to represent the values of the revolution. During this honeymoon period, content mattered much less than contentment. The popularity of change also spelled doom for parties representing the golden past. Often led by octogenarians from the prewar party leadership, these groupings – like the Independent Smallholders in Hungary or the Bulgarian Agrarian National Union in Bulgaria – received a relatively small percentage of the vote. A high turnout (Hungary's was the lowest at 63 percent – about the same as had voted in Poland the previous spring) also indicated enthusiasm for the process of change.

The rise and fall of heroes

The victors in these elections were giants of national stature. Some had more opposition credentials than others; all appeared to confer credibility, stability, and power upon the country. A look at this pantheon of heroes offers a contrast to the age that came later. Thus Lech Wałęsa: once an electrician at the Lenin Shipyard in Gdańsk, his leadership in Solidarity had made him the most recognizable Polish oppositionist, and earned him the Nobel Peace Prize in 1983. He shepherded the round table and election processes, while declining himself to run for office. By mid-1990, the sense in Poland was that conditions had changed since Jaruzelski's election as president; Wałęsa himself let it be known that he was ready. Jaruzelski stepped down graciously, and (after a contentious election, to be discussed below), Wałęsa became president that December. For the next five years, he would be the bane of *bien-pensant* Poles: a gifted strategist who enjoyed great respect abroad, but also an unpredictable figure, prone to embarrassing missteps and maybe harboring dreams of riding in on a white horse to save his country from the woes of democracy.

One of the reasons Wałęsa wanted to be president – and why Poland, too, wanted him in 1990 – was because of Havel's success in Czechoslovakia. That Havel could single-handedly raise his country's prestige – addressing, for example, a joint session of the US Congress – led Poles to feel they had been left behind, stuck with an old communist leader. A similar emotion propelled change in Bulgaria, where the reformist Socialist Party president Petar Mladenov, who had succeeded Zhivkov in November 1989, lasted only until July 1990, when a wave of student protest brought Zhelyu Zhelev to power (elected by Parliament). Zhelev, a philosopher, was famous for authoring a book on fascism, which – published by accident in 1982, then recalled – was a thinly veiled critique of Zhivkov's regime. In 1988, he had co-founded one of Bulgaria's first opposition movements, the Ruse Committee, which raised environmental issues. Though less well-known than Havel, he projected a similar image of moral and political authority.

In Hungary, the role of patron was filled by Árpád Göncz – a playwright like Havel, sentenced to life imprisonment after the 1956 revolution. Göncz, at first, was seen as a controversial figure, as he represented a party rivaling that of Prime Minister Antall. Constitutional amendments in 1991 reduced his role to that of figurehead; he served ten full years, acquiring a reputation as a moral voice above the fray and a representative of Hungarian national values. In the Baltics, the foremost figure was Vytautas Landsbergis, one of the founders of the Sajūdis Movement for Reform. A musicologist, Landsbergis was chosen as president by the Lithuanian Soviet on March 11, 1990, the day Lithuania declared its independence of the USSR.

Even Franjo Tudjman belongs in this category. Like the others, he had been punished for his dissident actions, spending several years in prison for advocacy of Croatian nationalism. He shared with the rest (except Wałęsa) credentials as a scholar of the humanities. He was the same age as Göncz; as a (self-taught) historian, he imparted gravity to the Croatian cause. Tudjman departed from his presidential peers as he imposed authoritarian rule on Croatia both during the war and after.

Another type of national leader in this period came from the ranks of senior communists who made the astute decision to abandon their internationalist faith for the national cause. Slobodan Milošević is here a poor example: his nationalism appeared in the end to be primarily about personal power. Better examples are Milan Kučan of Slovenia (1990–2002) and Kiro Gligorov of Macedonia (1991–99). Both were members of the communist elite under Tito (Gligorov old enough to have fought in World War Two; Kučan a generation younger); both had learned how to maneuver diplomatically in defense of their republics. Indeed, as Milošević's career track reveals, Tito's Yugoslavia was an excellent school for politicians. As Yugoslavia fell apart, both developed, reluctantly at first, a moderate nationalism. Because neither republic had plausible designs on its neighbors, neither man had the chance or inclination to become a Tudjman, nor suffer the misfortunes of Bosnian Alija Izetbegović; Kučan's encounter with the robust civil society of Ljubljana in the late 1980s made him a democrat, something which came harder in Macedonia. Gligorov's age and the respect he enjoyed abroad made him something of a Tito figure, especially after he survived a car-bomb attack in October 1995.

During the early post-revolution years, these father figures were indispensable, reminding their nations of the recent struggles while giving their countries international voices. Most also provided the glue that held together grand coalitions of national renewal, briefly uniting right, center, and the (non-communist) left. Within a year after the revolutions, though, these coalitions began to come apart, while the giants themselves showed some impatience. The results were a real test of democracy.

Poland's Solidarity coalition had already started to fray by the spring of 1990. Shock therapy put enormous strains on society and caused the government's popularity to plummet. Meanwhile, debates about national symbols, such as whether the Polish eagle should wear a crown, and whether that crown should have a cross, exposed deep divisions among Solidarity politicians. Wałęsa began to call for a "war at the top" to decide the country's direction. A series of vicious confrontations with his old allies showed that he no longer had any use for the left-liberal intellectual traditions of Solidarity. Ultimately, Wałęsa decided to run for president – against the prime minister. That election, in November 1990, destroyed the myth of Solidarity, and its broad social consensus. Mazowiecki suffered a humiliating defeat: he was placed third, behind an eccentric émigré, Stan Tyminski, who brandished (but never opened) a black briefcase containing a "secret plan" to save Poland. The election broke open the political system. Soon, there were dozens of major parties, and Wałęsa became even more dominant. His power peaked in 1992, when he dismissed the government of Jan Olszewski – barely eight months after Poland's first fully democratic parliamentary elections – in the wake of the secret-police files scandal discussed earlier. Even out of office, Wałęsa has continued to speak the part of a reluctant national savior.

Over the years, Bulgaria's Zhelyu Zhelev played a role quite similar to that of Wałęsa. Eighteen months after becoming president, Zhelev was elected again, this time by popular vote, and with the backing of the Union of Democratic Forces that he had helped found. The UDF was a broad anti-communist coalition, whose members ranged from the Podkrepa trade union and the green dissident group Ekoglasnost to conservative nationalist groupings.[4] The conflict between the

UDF and its former leader seemed like that between the Solidarity government and Wałęsa. The first UDF government, coincidentally, was elected the same month as that of Olszewski in Poland. Filip Dimitrov's tenure as prime minister lasted about as long, and fell for the same reasons. Dimitrov pursued the former communist elite vigorously, with a ferocity that alarmed Zhelev and some of the UDF's allies, including the Turkish party, the Movement for Rights and Freedoms. The president came to fear that decommunization would tear the country apart, and lose allies; in August 1992, he sharply criticized the government. The MRF withdrew its support, and the government fell in October. As in Poland, the result was a moderating of anti-communism, as well as of economic reform. Meanwhile the "dark blue" (from its original campaign color) UDF, like Solidarity, moved to the right, in this case purging members with any communist ties. By 1993, the UDF was calling unsuccessfully on Zhelev to resign, for having overstepped the limits of his supposedly ceremonial office. Like Wałęsa, Zhelev served but one term; the UDF refused to renominate him in the election of 1996.

The honeymoon ended most dramatically in Czechoslovakia; though his tenure in office was twice as long, Havel failed where his colleagues elsewhere succeeded. His problem was the Czech ambivalence toward dissidents, and toward the communist era as a whole. Repressive countries that had had a very small anti-communist opposition, such as Bulgaria or the Baltic states, might later be inclined to reward the very few brave enough to have spoken up; where the opposition had been large and open, as in Poland or even Hungary, voters could almost require an opposition pedigree. Czechoslovakia fell in between: the opposition had been large enough to show dissent was possible, but was in the end a small elite. Even before he became president, Havel raised citizens' ire by apologizing for the treatment of Germans after World War Two. His political group, Civic Forum – formed during the Velvet Revolution – swept the first free elections in June 1990, but President Havel soon made himself unpopular. His cautious stance on lustration (though he did not prevent laws from being enacted) brought charges of being soft on communism, while his calls for renewed morality seemed irrelevant or otherworldly. The sharpest conflict was with Václav Klaus, Finance Minister from 1989 and Czech Prime Minister from 1992 to to 1997. Klaus first destroyed Civic Forum, taking control and then abruptly, in late 1990, forming the Civic Democratic Party, which soon became the most popular party on a platform of lustration and Thatcherite economic change. While Zhelev and Wałęsa had been able to hold on to the center against such challenges from the right, Havel could not. This is probably due in large part to the splitting of Czechoslovakia, which distracted Havel at a crucial time, and pushed him to the margins as president of a country he did not want.

The role of all three of these leaders (to which one could add Kučan in Slovenia, and perhaps Göncz in Hungary) was nicely captured by Wałęsa, who spoke of balance: a country needed a strong right leg and a strong left leg, he often remarked; his job was to make up for the weakness of either leg. During the first three or so years of the post-communist era, this strategy prevented a frenzied witch hunt against the communists; it also, most likely, allowed the communist successor parties (with the exception of the Czech communists) to moderate, and to find their way in the new political landscape. At the same time, though, they represented another era, though the youngest of them (Wałęsa and Kučan) were around fifty when communism fell. To an extent that was both valuable and ultimately limiting, they judged situations with yardsticks inherited from their years opposing communism. Still, their second act as political moderates was as important, and more surprising, than their revolutionary first act.

Return of the communists

Revolutionary approaches, in fact, were what brought down the first liberal governments. They pushed hard on economic reform – believing they had a brief window of opportunity – and tried to overhaul the political system rapidly, too. The honeymoon period may have been real, yet it was, in retrospect, unrealistic to expect that East Europeans would patiently turn their fates over to a new regime of experts, no matter how well-intentioned. Intellectual dissidents for the most part turned out to be poor communicators, too. After a few years of this, voters in the emerging democracies looked for alternatives. Was this immaturity, or the opposite? The choice voters made was not for radically different policies, but for a different style.

The first defeat of the liberals was the most shocking. Lithuania had begun its fight to free itself from the Soviet Union in 1988, led by Sąjūdis. Sąjūdis pressed for independence and political change, and had been rewarded with over 70 percent of the seats for candidates it backed in elections to the Lithuanian Supreme Soviet in February 1990. Days later, the republic's government declared independence. For almost two more years, Lithuania remained nominally in the Soviet Union, but the prestige of Landsbergis and Sąjūdis seemed only to grow. Then, in October 1992, voters returned the communists, now renamed the Lithuanian Democratic Labor Party, to power, with just over half the seats in Parliament. Just five months later Algirdas Brazauskas, who had led the Lithuanian Communist Party and its successor since 1988, was elected president, with 60 percent of the vote.

Lithuanians, it is true, had had little experience with democracy in their entire history. But Brazauskas, a supporter of economic reform and of Lithuanian independence, was a practical choice. Landsbergis, like Wałęsa in Poland, had acquired a reputation as a mercurial power-broker who didn't hesitate to brandish the fear of communist resurgence. Economic reform took a heavy toll on Lithuanians, with energy shortages plaguing the country. Many voters may have hoped that Brazauskas and his party would be better at bargaining with Russia, still Lithuania's largest trading partner. Ultimately, they chose experience over confrontation.

Nowhere had the communists enjoyed less respect, by 1989, than in Poland. The party had almost disappeared in 1981, as Poles flocked to the Solidarity alternative. Social movements of the 1980s had held up the communists to merciless ridicule. True, careful reading of the results of the June 1989 elections would show that millions of voters had freely chosen communist candidates, but the party's rebirth as the Social Democratic Party of the Republic of Poland netted it only 60,000 members of the 2–3 million it had boasted in the 1980s.[5] And yet, in September 1993, the Social Democrats won 20 percent of the votes and 37 percent of the seats in Parliament's lower house; their coalition partner, the Polish Peasant Party (heirs to a communist-era puppet party), gave them a solid majority.

Negative explanations abounded: the right was splintered by acrimony after the secret-police files débâcle, and could not agree on common platforms or coalitions. The post-Solidarity center, meanwhile, had nothing new to offer, four years after 1989; it retained the architects of shock therapy, and could not win back the support of trade unions, who had come to see economic reform as threatening not only their jobs, but their entire way of life. But the victorious Social Democrats deserve much credit. After several years of unstable governments and fractious parliaments, they promised calm, continuity, and responsiveness: "It doesn't have to be this way any more – reforms should work for people" was a prominent slogan.[6] Party leaders projected images of youthfulness (some were too young to have played much of a role before 1989), competence, and concern for those harmed by change. The message was decidedly not populist; nor did the Social Democrats promise to roll back reforms. The next four years, indeed, saw a general continuation of liberal economic reform and strong economic growth, combined with attention to the widening holes in the social safety-net, pensions in particular. While the Social Democrats did not solve these problems, they did put them on the table. What is particularly striking is that they did not simply attract the votes of the disaffected; instead, their support came rather evenly from all social groups, and from first-time voters as well as old party stalwarts.[7]

Nor did voters have second thoughts about having tossed out Solidarity. Two years later, the presidential campaign pitted Wałęsa – who had tried hard to undermine the leftist governments, most vigorously in the closing hours of his presidency with allegations (never proven) that Prime Minister Józef Oleksy had spied for the KGB – against Social Democratic leader Aleksander Kwaśniewski. Wałęsa made the campaign a choice between the communist past and the Solidarity future, but voters looked to Kwaśniewski and saw the future in him instead. Like his younger Social Democratic colleagues (he resigned from the party in order to run), Kwaśniewski projected managerial competence, youth, and openness. Many who voted for him had fought hard to bring down communism in the

1980s; once again, they rejected an unresponsive leader in favor of progress.

In retrospect, it was not surprising that the ex-communists should return to power in Hungary. There, only those over fifty, who had witnessed the crushing of the 1956 revolution, had directly negative experience of communist rule. Subsequent generations had welcomed the mantra of party leader János Kádár: "He who is not against us is with us." Hungarian Socialist Workers Party ranks were open to a technocratic intelligentsia with minimal interest in proletarian dictatorship; in 1989, that elite had yielded to social pressures relatively easily. Though that benevolent image did not prevent an embarrassing result in 1990, the renamed Hungarian Socialist Party was well positioned to remake itself into a democratic competitor.

As in Poland, the first democratic government did itself no favors. It found itself trapped between liberal "shock therapy" advocates, never dissatisfied with the pace of economic change, on the one hand, and nationalists (like István Csurka, or József Torgyán of the Independent Smallholders) who railed against foreign investors and advocated instead radical redistribution of national wealth. When Prime Minister Antall died in December 1993, his successor, Péter Boross, chose to pander to the right, with, for example, harsh legislation punishing crimes of the communist era, or preventing foreign land-ownership. As Wałęsa would do in 1995, the HDF tried to make the May 1994 parliamentary elections a referendum on the communist era – relentlessly attacking the socialist leader Gyula Horn for having been an enthusiastic communist student activist in 1956. The result was unequivocal: the HDF lost fully half of its support to come in third place, while support for the socialists more than tripled, to 33 percent (and a majority of seats in Parliament). And while post-dissident parties elsewhere treated former communists as radioactive, Hungary's Alliance of Free Democrats joined the socialists in a coalition government.

It is possible to see what one wants to see in the ex-communist parties' success. To put it down to a murky combination of misplaced nostalgia and voter inexperience, though, skirts the issue. Nor, surprisingly, did the rebuilt communist parties learn from their Western comrades and mobilize those hurt by free market reforms.

Both nostalgia and Old Left rhetoric (somewhat disguised) did win some voters, but would not have been nearly enough for electoral victory. Nor is it sufficient to dwell on the failures of the post-dissident parties, either – to suggest that if only they had managed better, the ex-communists would never have had a chance. In truth, the competing challenges of economic and political reconstruction were such that no party was likely to maintain power for very long. Given the foibles of those first post-revolutionary governments, it would not be hard to present one's party as an alternative.

The wonder, though, is that in none of the cases mentioned (to which one could add the success of the former communists in Bulgaria, Macedonia, Romania, and Slovenia) did voters opt for the populist alternative. Instead, they largely chose to stay the course in terms of economic change. The most significant difference between the parties victorious in 1992–94 and their predecessors was not in economic terms; if anything, they were slightly more liberal than the governments they succeeded, though that was not obvious to all of their electorate. The contrast was greatest in national policy. Especially in Hungary, Poland, and Croatia (after Tudjman's fall), nationalism – and invocation of faith – proved to be an electoral platform with surprisingly short legs. Nationalism, after all, had been part of communist regime policy, too; while East Europeans welcomed the opportunity to explore national culture without ideological strictures, they also recoiled at government attempts to engineer cultural tastes. So too, while they had demanded freedom of religious worship in 1989, efforts of church leaders to back one party over another did not help, whether in Catholic, Orthodox, Protestant, or Muslim countries.

Finally, though the pattern of former communists returning to power has repeated itself almost everywhere (with only the Czech Republic, Estonia, and Latvia as holdouts), this fact conceals two separate trends. In those countries where civil society was most developed, an organized opposition had exerted real pressure on the ruling communist regimes, forcing them to change. The result was that, by 1990, these communist parties had – whether out of pragmatism, cunning, or genuine evolution – become social democrats of one kind or another, and were ready to compete in the democratic forum. This is not to say that they would be free from corruption, incompetence, and populist temptations, but only that they became normal parties with some inconvenient baggage.

Elsewhere, the trend was similar to that in Russia or in other post-Soviet states: the communists really never gave up power in the first place. The fall of communism was in these cases only a temporary setback, necessitating a revamping of party image. Here, the classic example is Serbia's Milošević; others followed his lead. These leaders and their parties simply became nationalist chauvinists, and found the ideology quite compatible. Like communism, exclusive nationalism privileges a collective identity in opposition to those excluded (for reasons of class or national allegiance). Both ideologies easily accommodate a powerful, charismatic leader, centralized power, economic autarky, and tightly controlled media. Surviving 1989 intact, in societies where a civic opposition had not really developed, would not prove at all difficult.

Four last dictators

From the perspective of political change, '1989' is in many cases an inaccurate shorthand; the real end to authoritarian rule would take another decade. The fall of second-generation authoritarian governments in 1997–2000 was at times no less dramatic than the events of 1989. Four cases – Slovakia, Romania, Croatia, and Serbia – each show, paradoxically, how much harder it was for a democratic opposition to succeed when the repression of the communist era gave way to a soft dictatorship that offered a program of xenophobic nationalism and crony capitalism. The ethnopolitical tug has been strong, and remains the greatest threat to democracy in the region.

Slovaks had organized a vibrant underground opposition to communism, and built a thriving civil society in the first post-communist years. Yet by 1996 Slovakia was a country where political murders and kidnappings had become ordinary tools, and where the prime minister and his cronies mobilized the masses and manipulated Parliament and the media to intimidate or silence opponents. This was in some ways the most disheartening story in the region, as it showed how nationalist populism could undermine democracy even where it had seemed strong.

The root of Slovakia's political crisis lay in the Velvet Divorce. The break-up of Czechoslovakia was not popularly driven, but rather dictated by the ambitions of a few politicians in Prague and Bratislava. Backing into independence, Slovakia lost its way forward. Vladimír Mečiar had won his battle for independence, yet given the smug satisfaction of Czech politicians like Václav Klaus, it was hard not to see that Slovakia had also been humiliated. The Slovak economy was weak, its international position (including its relationship with Hungary, as well as with the Czech Republic) uncertain. Prime Minister Mečiar appeared to have no idea how to proceed after the divorce was final. In the end, his promise to make Slovakia a great country proved less important than the amassing of political power.

Though the opposition parties were more inclined to quarrel with one another than to develop alternative visions of Slovakia's future, they did succeed, in March 1994, in passing a vote of no confidence in Mečiar's government. This success was short-lived; in parliamentary elections that September, Mečiar's Movement for a Democratic Slovakia (MDS) ran a classic populist campaign (with funding from like-minded Silvio Berlusconi's Forza Italia), promising "jobs, prosperity, peace, order and opportunity for everybody."[8] Winning 35 percent of the vote, the MDS controlled Parliament in a "red–brown" (that is, ex-communist left and nationalist right) coalition with the Association of Workers of Slovakia (which received, in the new government, the privatization ministry) and the Slovak National Party. Now Mečiar moved to cement his power. He turned on President Michal Kováč, a former MDS member elected by Parliament in 1993 who had since shown a willingness to veto laws and to criticize Mečiar's policies. Mečiar announced that the election had ended Kováč's mandate. When Kováč refused to step down, Parliament nearly voted to dismiss him (with just under the three-fifths majority required by the constitution), on the basis of a secret report accusing him of conspiring to overthrow the government. Three months later, shortly before Kováč's annual State of the Republic address, the State Intelligence Service engineered the abduction and torture of the president's son; Michal Kováč Jr was found outside an Austrian police station, and then spent six months in jail as part of an Interpol fraud investigation. Government-controlled media suggested that the Kováč duo had engineered the kidnapping themselves. As the investigation nevertheless came closer and closer to Mečiar, an intelligence officer with information about the case was killed by a car-bomb.

Mečiar's fall in 1998 may not qualify as a revolution, but it did rescue Slovakia from its pathetic descent into isolation. When President Kováč's term ended in March 1998, Parliament's deadlock on a successor gave presidential powers to the prime minister. Mečiar promptly issued blanket amnesties for the Kováč abduction and other crimes, and pushed through Parliament laws designed to widen his power. This time, the opposition united and emerged victorious in the September 1998 elections. The new government of Mikuláš Dzurinda has worked ever since to undo Mečiar's legacy, with great success; Mečiar himself lost in Slovakia's first direct presidential election, in 1999 – but with over 40 percent of the vote, and repeated that result in 2004. Though most Slovaks now regard him as dangerous, even psychologically unbalanced, he remains one of the country's most popular politicians.

Given the total control that communist leader Nicolae Ceauşescu exerted over Romania – control unmatched except in Albania – democratic emergence after his overthrow would have been remarkable. The mobilization of miners, now in support of President Ion Iliescu, now against, in the first two post-communist years revealed an unsettled society, distrustful of formal politics. President Iliescu won his first term, in 1990, with 85 percent of the vote, and claimed 61 percent two years later. Like Mečiar, Iliescu's problem was finding a vision for the country that went beyond xenophobia (attacks on Radio Free Europe, for example) and a vague social democracy; he found it in the power of his National Salvation Front. For the first seven years, Iliescu dominated Romanian politics, ruling above the constitution and behind the scenes of successive governments. He emphasized the threats ethnic Romanians faced from the Hungarian minority and from the predatory capitalist West. The opposition, in turn, relied on a program of anti-communism and charges of corruption and conspiracy. Only in 1996 was there a real change of government, as Emil Constantinescu and his Democratic Convention of Romania, a liberal coalition based in the urban middle class, found a positive, cohesive message allowing them to sweep the presidential and parliamentary elections. One term proved too short to root out the endemic corruption and to overcome deep national antipathies; in 2000, Iliescu returned to power with nearly 70 percent of the vote (over extremist Corneliu Vadim Tudor, in an echo of the Polish presidential election of 1990), while his Social Democrats dominated the Parliament. The December 2004 elections, however, have hastened the end of a long era of quasi-democratic communism. Credible accusations of fraud (such as busloads of multiple voters) by Iliescu's team marred the election, but a vibrant independent media swept Traian Băsescu, Mayor of Bucharest and a former ship's captain, to a narrow victory over Iliescu's candidate, the sitting prime minister. Băsescu oversaw the formation of a government focused on preparing Romania for entry to the European Union.

If Slovakia and Romania drifted toward authoritarian rule as an ill-prepared citizenry lent support to directionless populist leaders, Croatia and Serbia plunged directly into dictatorship: national chauvinism and wartime discipline brought Franjo Tudjman and Slobodan Milošević to power, and made them almost impossible to defeat. A macabre joke circulating in Croatia in 1998–99 asked which animal could save Croatia. The cruel answer – which neatly captured the opposition's helplessness – was the crab (*rak*), which in Croatian is also the word for cancer. Tudjman's death from stomach cancer in December 1999 indeed liberated Croatia from an increasingly rigid dictatorship. Serbia's liberation the following year would require much greater sacrifice.

Throughout the four years of the Croatian and Bosnian wars, Tudjman's position was unassailable. His international reputation, to be sure, was that of an old-fashioned irredentist. British MP Paddy Ashdown – years later appointed international administrator in Bosnia-Hercegovina – found himself seated next to Tudjman in 1995 at a dinner in London marking the fiftieth anniversary of V-E Day. Tudjman grabbed a paper napkin and drew for Ashdown his plan for Bosnia: a line dividing it neatly between parts to be annexed to Croatia and to Serbia. Tudjman's praise for leaders of the wartime fascist state and his efforts to minimize Croatia's role in the Holocaust had gained him great notoriety by that time, too.

Yet, at home, Tudjman was still a national hero. Just as he celebrated the expulsion of the Serbs from Krajina, in 1995, however, he faced a challenge. As he had done in 1992, when the fighting in Bosnia was at its height, he called early elections, hoping to ride the wave of this military victory. The results were mixed: Tudjman's Croatian Democratic Union again won the majority, but was badly beaten in local elections. In Zagreb and other cities, the opposition swept city councils. Meanwhile, independent media – led by the weekly *Feral Tribune* in Split – stepped up its ridicule of President Tudjman's pompous authoritarianism. Tudjman and his party lashed back: he refused to accept Zagreb's choice for mayor, and, after a long stalemate, simply dissolved the City Council and appointed his own. In 1996, a new law made it a crime to criticize high officials; *Feral Tribune* (which combined outrageous pornography-laced satire with courageous reporting) was the first to be charged. Tudjman's move to shut down a popular independent radio station in late 1996 brought tens of thousands to the streets in protest.

By the time of Tudjman's death, Croatia had come to be seen in the same category as Milošević's Serbia. Elections held one month later, in January 2000, brought a surprise defeat for his party. A coalition of the former communists and a party largely representing liberal intellectuals won decisively; Stipe Mesić, once a member of the last Yugoslav collective presidency, then a Tudjman ally, but who had long since broken with him over the latter's aggressive national-ism, was elected president. The results appeared remarkable, but in fact marked Croatia's abrupt emergence into normal democratic alternation. The coalition was much like that which has governed Croatia's neighbor Hungary off and on; as in Hungary, Croatian voters appear to prefer alternating between social-liberal govern-ments that promote economic reform over national chauvinism, and much-moderated nationalists, who promise a national renaissance and a restoration of the social safety-net.

No ruler had greater staying power in the post-communist era than Slobodan Milošević. By the end of 1999, he had survived no fewer than four lost wars. Ultimately, what brought him down was a popular uprising that not only was the largest demonstration of civil society activism in Eastern Europe since 1989; it has also been an inspiration for democracy movements in Ukraine and elsewhere in the last few years.

Serbs had several opportunities to remove Milošević from power. In March 1991, massive demonstrations on the streets of Belgrade seemed to spell the end for his rule. These demonstrations, it has to be said, were not the equivalent of those that toppled communism elsewhere in 1989. They originated in a rally of Vuk Drasković's Serbian Renewal Movement, protesting the regime's manipulation of the media. But Drasković, at the time, was attacking Milošević from a more nationalist position; he compared Milošević to Ceauşescu, and suggested that Milošević and his wife Mirjana Milošević would meet the same fate.[9] Demonstrators called for democratic reform, but they also sang long-banned Serbian nationalist songs as they built barricades and took over the city center. In response, Milošević sent in riot police and then the army. Several demonstrators were killed, and Drasković (who had run against Milošević in presidential elections the year before) was briefly arrested. Milošević then faced down the student demonstrators, and won their support.

Five years later, the protests were even more determined. By the winter of 1996–97, the dream of a Greater Serbia was in a shambles, and economic sanctions had turned life in "rump Yugoslavia" into a shadow of normalcy. That November, an opposition coalition, Zajedno (Together) won local elections across Serbia. Zoran Djindjić, leader of the Democratic Party, was elected mayor of Belgrade. Milošević annulled the results, prompting instant demonstrations in Belgrade. This time, democratic rhetoric outstripped the nationalist voice in the demonstrations, which now had a much more carnivalesque feel to them. For three full months, tens of thousands gathered every day to blow whistles and bang on pots while calling for the elections to be recognized. It seemed as if the people had won, but Milošević was again able to hold on to power. After sending in the riot police (the army this time would not be deployed), he gave in, quietly, and recognized opposition victories. But Zajedno proved intractably disunited, and failed to push for the realization of other demands, such as loosened restrictions on the media and the universities. The coalition soon broke apart: later in 1997, Drasković's party ejected Djindjić from the mayoralty. Milošević was left free to accumulate more power – he moved from the Serbian presidency to the safer presidency of still-federal Yugoslavia.

Even the débâcle of Kosovo did not topple Milošević; the NATO bombing of Belgrade, echoing as it did Nazi Germany's destruction of the same city fifty-eight years earlier, served in part to confirm what Milošević had claimed all along: the West was out to get Serbs. Some recognized that only without Milošević could the country hope to escape the spiral of destruction, deprivation, and repression. Hoping to capitalize on the lingering post-Kosovo sense of national unity, Milošević arranged for the constitution to be amended, allowing for direct election of the president, and scheduled the elections for September. Despite his growing unpopularity, he could still, it was believed, count on the opposition's disarray.

Into the breach stepped Otpor (Resistance). This movement began at the universities in 1998; two years later its graffiti and posters were ubiquitous parts of the Serbian urban landscape. So, too, was its determination familiar. Like their predecessors in Poland or Czechoslovakia a dozen years earlier, the students of Otpor were willing to go to jail for their right to speak, and professed an unshaken commitment to the principles of non-violence. Otpor began sending simple care packages to Yugoslav soldiers, in hopes of bridging the rifts created by Milošević's culture of war. They also recognized that a regime could look foolish and vindictive when it arrested and tortured high-school or university students for wearing T-shirts or passing out leaflets; and that, as students, they could risk jail without risking jobs or families. Their language was subtle ridicule: in one "happening" (to use the term popularized in late-communist Poland), Otpor activists distributed leaflets to people waiting in long lines for basic food items; the simple slogan on the leaflet read "Are you OK?" which also means "Are you in line?" in Serbian.[10] Thus, ordinary people were forced to decide whether they were in fact satisfied with economic deprivation, and to think about the courage of those who would ask about their well-being in this way.

As the election approached, Otpor decided to support the opposition, no matter what; activists worked to recruit voters individually. Their posters now read "He is finished." A self-fulfilling prophecy: with Otpor assuming the role of the nation's conscience – and with the United States, among others, putting pressure on the opposition to stop squabbling – Vojislav Koštunica emerged as Milošević's nemesis. A lawyer who combined solid opposition credentials with a firm, but not aggressive, nationalism, Koštunica appeared to many Serbs to restore honesty and integrity to the Serbian nation. Milošević waged an ugly, violent campaign, which included the kidnapping and murder, just weeks before the elections, of Ivan Stambolić, who had once been his patron in the League of Communists but was now an outspoken critic. Nevertheless, a clear majority of Serbs and Montenegrins voted for Koštunica. Milošević was finished.

Except not quite yet. As the results poured in, Milošević ordered them fixed; the Central Election Commission duly announced that Koštunica had not quite received 50 percent and ordered a run-off election. Rather than acquiesce in this charade, Koštunica, the opposition, and Otpor instead stepped up calls for Milošević to resign, while the military and police quietly moved toward neutrality. On October 5, 2000, a massive crowd of demonstrators from all over Yugoslavia – including thousands of miners in their work clothes and, famously, the mayor of the city of Čačak, who arrived with a convoy of bulldozers – gathered before the National Assembly. The police melted away, and Koštunica was able to address the crowd: "Good evening, liberated Serbia."

That moment could stand as a fitting end to a century of cruel European dictatorships, and perhaps also as a coda to the fall of communism. But a careful reader will have noticed that these authoritarian regimes were not typical. In each country, there were opposition parties ready to take power when the leader finally faltered; there were civic movements fighting for human rights and standing up despite repression; and independent media – radio especially, but also newspapers – continued to present alternative perspectives, for those who cared or dared to listen. The problem was that, for most of the 1990s, the majority in each country did support Mečiar, or Iliescu, or Tudjman, or Milošević. The pull of national pride was stronger than the appeal of pluralism.

One is reminded rather of Poland and Hungary in the 1980s. There, too, communist authoritarianism survived through a mixture of confused benevolence toward a growing opposition and everhollower appeals to nationalism, while a state monopoly on the media hid a pluralist underground beneath. As the end had come easily in 1989, so it would in the 1990s. Hubris proved no less the bane of these mini-dictators than it had for the democratic politicians elsewhere in the region. With Milošević's fall, Eastern Europe turned a page.

It would be an exaggeration, though, to suggest that the fall of Milošević ushered in an age of democracy and liberty across Eastern Europe. Indeed, less than two and a half years later, Serbian Prime Minister Zoran Djindjić was assassinated – felled by a sniper's bullet in the parking lot of the main government building in Belgrade. Djindjić, one of the heroes of October 2000, had spent much of his administration clashing with President Kostunica, whom he saw as obstructing Serbia's efforts to win the support of the international community. On the other side of the right, Djindjić sought to gain control over the nationalist paramilitary groups that had a stranglehold on Serbian politics. Hardened in the Croatian, Bosnian, and Kosovan wars, they returned home to shore up Milošević's power. The most feared paramilitary leader, Željko "Arkan" Raznatović was himself assassinated in the lobby of a Belgrade hotel in January 2000. Many others continued to find Belgrade and Serbia a safe haven. One of these, Milorad Luković (called "Legija" for his service in the French Legion) had cooperated with Djindjić to bring about Milošević's downfall in 2000. When Djindjić prepared to strengthen control over the police and army, he paid with his life.

Consulting the department of specious statistics, we could compare the last fifteen years to Eastern Europe in the years between the World Wars, and note that three assassinations of national leaders (Stambolić and Djindjić in Serbia, in 2000 and 2003, and former Bulgarian Prime Minister Andrei Lukanov, in 1996; there was also the attempted assassination of Macedonian President Gligorov), and just three governments toppled amid social unrest (Bulgaria 1997, Albania 1997, Serbia 2000), is a great improvement. More seriously, one should ask why there is such a gap between the now-established democratic practices north of the Danube and the woeful failures to the south – and might such differences be permanent?

This question is a part of one of the most important riddles about the world today: Why are some places democracies, and others not, and can democracy be created anywhere? One approach to an answer – most recently identified with the work of the political scientist Samuel Huntington – considers long-term cultural traditions to be the key. Eastern Orthodox Christianity in the Balkans (and Russia), the theory goes, has had limited access to the forces of humanism, the Enlightenment, the Industrial Revolution, and political democracy. These countries (like those of the Arab world) simply belong to a different civilization, one which until now has never developed a vocabulary of democratic politics.[11]

Recent Eastern European history shows the limits of this idea: Croatia, for example, did not represent a "Western" alternative to "Eastern" Serbia in its war; nor can the Bosnian War be understood as such a clash; the emergence of relatively stable democracies in the last few years in Bulgaria, Croatia, or Macedonia also calls into question the strength of cultural determinants. The medium past is also a problem: when Havel invoked Masaryk, he and many observers assumed that Czechs and Slovaks would benefit from their experience in the only Central European democracy to last until World War Two. Yet Czech democracy since 1989, though stable enough, has been rather less vibrant than that of its neighbors Hungary or Poland, despite their twentieth-century record of coups and dictatorships. In retrospect, it was foolish to expect that Czechoslovakia's elderly would inspire their grandchildren with fond memories of long-ago ballot boxes.

Another approach is to look at Western policies since 1989. Western democracies have supported countries they believe to be like them more than they have those that are further off and less familiar. And indeed, foreign investment (aside, of course, from military aid connected with the wars in Bosnia, Kosovo, or Afghanistan) has gone disproportionately to those countries near to and similar to those of Western donors. Geographic proximity to Western Europe goes a long way toward predicting the success of economic and political change. The forces of democratic change are obviously transnational – money, information, and expertise moving across borders – as well as domestic.[12]

Both these explanations require us to think about the legacies of the past. Rather than reaching to the distant past that may or may not erect civilizational barriers, or might prejudice would-be donors, let us focus here on recent legacies, which augur best for democratic change. The places where stable democratic politics took hold by 1995 – the Baltic states, the Czech and Slovak republics, Hungary, Poland, and Slovenia – were also those where civil-society opposition to communism emerged earliest, and was quite well developed by 1989. Elsewhere, intellectual dissent was common, but did not reach much beyond discussion circles or the reformist wing of the ruling Communist Party. Civil-society opposition was, in turn, more or less prepared to adopt a democratic culture (or to recognize the value in doing so), while the voting population was more or less prepared to accept the compromises and disagreements associated with such a political system. (Of course, long-term cultural traditions, ranging from education to the private ownership of land, play a role here, too; nevertheless, the short-term historical legacies, too often over-looked, are of particular importance. Those recent factors, after all, exert a more direct influence on the individuals who participate in political life today.)

The revolutions of 1989, then, set some countries directly on the path to political democracy. Others were far behind, but would begin a similar journey that has yet to reach that same endpoint. The best example of this is Serbia. Like Poland or Hungary before 1989, Milošević's regime was a hybrid: a dictatorship, with plenty of opponents in exile, in prison, or prudently silent; but also a messy place, where some independent media (like the radio station B-92) and social movements (human rights groups, for example) could manage to survive. Yet as in the communist regimes, it was extraordinarily difficult to develop the kind of reasoning that makes a democracy succeed in the face of populist pressures. In Belgrade during the 1996 protests, Lawrence Weschler encountered urban youth staging inventive, carnivalesque demonstrations, as if it were 1989 again. "Belgrade felt," he writes, "like a place the world has been repeatedly over the past generation: with a people rising up in joyous self-liberation as the regime's authority seemed magically to melt away. But this was not a place any of us have been before." He found instead what he called:

certain flaws in the Serbian operating system. Serbs didn't seem to understand, for instance, the notion that you couldn't believe both A and B if B had elements in it that were contrary to A. You had to *make up your mind.* They were not bound by the simple notion of the incompatibility of opposites, nor did they seem unduly bound by its corollary, the notion of consequence, the idea that if you believe X this might have implications for how you then have to behave in the world.[13]

Thus, Serbs could both loathe Milošević and still demand that Serbs not be blamed for the wars, or speak passionately about human rights while denying that the massacre at Srebrenica had taken place. Pride and national solidarity were clearly more important than tolerance, compromise, respect. The non-violent revolution of 2000, or the shocked response to Djindjić's assassination, may be steps toward a new political culture, one as different from the Serbian past as Poland or Hungary's current political system is from their pasts.

The same transformation can be seen in Romania or Croatia. The rampages of miners in Bucharest in 1990–91, or the fervent support for Franjo Tudjman's persecution of the Serbs (support which opponents such as Slavenka Drakulić and Dubravka Ugrešić lambasted in their essays)[14] have largely been replaced by the stuff of normal politics. Parties compete, and replace one another in government. Debates about economic reform and foreign policy have supplanted conflicts over Western influence, and the media have gained a great deal of independence. This is not to say that violent protest has disappeared. As recently as 1999, Romanian miners protesting threatened mine closures in the Jiu Valley took nearly two thousand policemen hostage, using them as human shields. Former Croatian soldiers have violently protested efforts to apprehend accused war criminals. Nor is the north free of such protest: in July 2005, thousands of Silesian miners descended on Warsaw to demand the continuation of a preferential pension plan. A violent clash with the police brought instant concessions from Parliament. But Eastern European politics now has less and less to distinguish it from politics in Western Europe.

The return of nationalist parties into power would seem to be an exception. When Ion Iliescu was reelected President of Romania in 2000, or when the Croatian Democratic Union (Tudjman's old party) won parliamentary elections in 2003, it seemed as if a new populist, xenophobic tide might destroy the progress those countries had made. In hindsight, though, there is an analogy with the return of post-communist parties to power in Poland and Hungary in the early 1990s. Yet Croatian Prime Minister Ivo Sanader appears to have little in common with his party's fire-breathing past. He won on promises to pay greater attention to living standards, even while continuing the reforms of the previous government. Again, hubris took its toll, as it had in Romania: governments (or parties) that were perceived to be out of touch with economic or social problems were rejected. But neither are rightist parties immune to this; nationalist slogans do not compensate for the absence of effective reform, as Iliescu and his party found out in 2004.

Two different ways of structuring power have crossed each other on the political map of post-communist Eastern Europe. One, which I have called here ethnopolitical, links the rights and benefits of citizenship to the nation. This is a zero-sum game, in which rights given to all destroy this connection. Majority-ethnicity parties by definition seek to control all political resources within their national group; minority groups can at best aspire to be apportioned some token representation, and at worst are placed outside of the citizenry. Often, the clash between majority and minority ethnopolitics can be resolved (or shunted on to a smaller stage) only by dividing the country.

Opposed to ethnopolitics is a politics based around differing interpretations of economic and social policy. The stakes are no lower in this politics, but they are subject to compromise. This politics, loosely based around the interests of different classes (though the lines are more blurred than they once were), has been shaped, in Eastern Europe, by the protest movements since the 1970s, and by civil society since 1989.[15] Conservative or liberal or social democratic parties succeed one another in most of the region now with some regularity; every time they do, they deepen the foundations of democracy.

What, then, is the place of politics in the lives of East Europeans? If the first post-revolutionary decade was about the movement *away* from communism (though that movement meant different things to different people), the next half-decade was about movement *toward* the European Union. The EU was not just a representation of Europe, but a club with highly demanding criteria. As countries began the journey toward membership, voters came to expect technocratic leadership, able to negotiate with EU leaders as equals. The post-communist era ended on the international stage, to which we now turn.

5 | A new Europe: the East in the West

Miklós Haraszti had two revelations for me as we settled down over coffee at the Le Meridien in Budapest one morning in early March 2003. First, he gazed around the lobby of this five-star hotel and remarked with a smile: "You can hardly recognize this place. I spent a lot of time here when this was police headquarters." Haraszti was one of Hungary's best-known political figures, and a leading representative (with Adam Michnik of Poland) of the post-1968 generation of anti-communist opposition. At one time, he had opposed communism from the left; his Marxist critiques of the dictatorship landed him in one of Hungary's last political trials. In the 1980s, he had articulated, both at home, and on the op-ed pages of Western newspapers, a vigorous defense of human and civic rights against tyranny. We speculated on whether my hotel room might have been once the scene of interrogations. Indeed, Budapest had changed, and the old was not to be missed.

When we had last met three years previously, Haraszti was deploring the right-wing stranglehold on politics and culture in Hungary. I knew no better observer of East European politics, and was eager to hear his take on the invasion of Iraq, then just days away. And that was the second surprise. He told me firmly that the West needed to take a stand against Saddam Hussein, and that the time for invasion had come.

Not only Haraszti, but the majority of the intellectual elites, and much of the middle class, in Hungary, the Czech Republic, Poland, and elsewhere felt strongly that the Iraq war was necessary. But the informed observer of Eastern Europe should rather ask why this support should come as a surprise. Eastern Europe's journey from Soviet domination toward an unexpected destination – a place which United States Secretary of Defense Donald Rumsfeld labeled the "New Europe," contrasting it to the Old Europe that sought to obstruct US plans to invade Iraq – may be the most remarkable development in the region since the millennium. The journey has been shaped by Western policies toward the region, to be sure, but also by a uniquely East European agenda born of the experience of leaving communism behind. For the first time in modern history, the region is not simply the subject of domination, but an independent and even influential actor. And for some, support for regime change in the Middle East became a logical conclusion to decades of struggle at home.

An "anachronistic straitjacket"

In terms of foreign relations, liberation in 1989 was at first not much more than a charade. On one side was a surprisingly reticent West. The policy of the United States under George H. W. Bush was not to commit too much support until it was clear "whether these reforms were real."[1] President Bush and Secretary of State James Baker reiterated then, and also two years later as the Soviet Union and Yugoslavia disintegrated, their preference for the status quo. Thus, for example, though the United States had never recognized Soviet annexation of the Baltic republics, it refrained from supporting their independence throughout 1990 and 1991. In Ukraine in August 1991, shortly before the attempted coup that would end the Soviet Union, Bush delivered what came to be known as his "chicken Kiev speech," warning that "suicidal nationalism" threatened progress in the Soviet Union. Baker echoed this line in Belgrade that same summer, urging the republics to negotiate.

The disappearance of the Iron Curtain raised the question, for Western leaders, of what would fill the vacuum left behind by the vacating power. They thus offered words of welcome, but little more. This wait-and-see attitude would, in the Yugoslav case, produce precisely what they had hoped to avoid: a rapid descent into bloody chaos. In 1990–91, it was already possible to see that the old regimes could not withstand the processes of change, but it was also difficult to imagine what might replace them.

The Warsaw Pact still existed, after all, as 1989 came to a close. The Communist Party still controlled the Soviet Union, and some 175,000 Soviet troops still were stationed in Czechoslovakia, Hungary, and

Poland (not to mention those in the Baltic republics, still part of the Soviet Union, and a further half-million in East Germany). To East Europeans, it was obvious that no change, domestic or international, could be permanent as long as the Soviet Army maintained its bases abroad. Mikhail Gorbachev had in 1988 annulled the Brezhnev doctrine – which held that the Soviet Union had a duty to defend socialism whenever it was threatened in an allied country (such as Czechoslovakia in 1968) – but who could say that Gorbachev was for ever?

For his part, Gorbachev did not expect that his "Sinatra doctrine" (a phrase coined by Foreign Ministry spokesman Gennadii Gerasimov, who mangled "I did it my way" into "they can do it their way") would erase the Soviet Army from Eastern Europe. Nevertheless, he adapted to this reality quickly. In this flexibility, he was constantly ahead of his Western counterparts. As early as December 1988, Gorbachev announced, in a speech to the UN General Assembly, that the USSR would withdraw from Eastern Europe (not including the Baltics) a half-million troops within two years. He envisioned a much smaller number remaining; early in 1990, it became clear that the new governments would not tolerate even a small presence.

The prospect of German unification changed everything. West German Chancellor Helmut Kohl introduced the prospect of a seemingly painless uniting of East and West in a December 1989 speech in Dresden, during the election campaign for the East German Parliament. East Germany was really the key to the whole Soviet presence in the region; Soviet policy toward Poland, for example, was usually understood to be dictated by the fact that Poland was a land bridge between the USSR and East Germany. By February, Gorbachev had accepted the eventual unification (with details to be worked out later), and the logic of empire evaporated. Soviet troops became an unjustifiable burden to their hosts.

First to sign an agreement was Czechoslovakia, in February 1990. Soviet troops had arrived there to crush the Prague Spring in August 1968, and had stayed ostensibly to guard against West German "revanchism." They numbered over 70,000, and were equipped with tactical nuclear weapons. Hungary's occupiers, in turn, had come to stay in 1944; Hungary had fought with the Axis powers, and was thus a defeated nation. The uprising of 1956 only confirmed the suspicions of the Soviets, who kept some 50,000 troops in Hungary through 1989. In both countries, desire to see the Soviet Army leave as quickly as possible was widely shared, even by reformist communists. Yet withdrawal brought new problems, more economic than military in nature. Soviet soldiers desperate to stay behind offered fantastic sums for arranged marriages. There were rumors of hand-grenades and small arms spilling out into local bazaars. Finally, negotiations over the value of Soviet occupation brought a pathetic end to what was supposedly a fraternal alliance. Soviet negotiators in both countries demanded compensation for the bases it had constructed, while the East Europeans retorted that most Soviet-constructed buildings were less than useless. The Mayor of Turnov, Czechoslovakia, suggested wryly that the Soviets could take the buildings with them: "they would not even have to tear some of them down, because they have already fallen apart."[2] Worse, as the troops left, the East Europeans slowly began to realize that they had been bequeathed dozens of ecological disasters; it was as if, Czech Prime Minister Petr Pithart remarked, the Soviets "had declared chemical warfare on us."[3]

Resentment of Soviet troops was even stronger in Poland and the Baltics, yet they found it harder to rid themselves of them. For Poland, home to 50,000 Soviet troops, German unification threatened to make Soviet disengagement a distant prospect. Moscow argued that the Soviet soldiers in East Germany, and their equipment, would have to cross Polish territory on their way home; Soviet troops in Poland would stay to monitor the process. It was easy enough to imagine a scenario of disgruntled, armed soldiers swarming off stalled trains on a looting spree – or even attempting (why not?) to return Poland to the Soviet fold. It would not be until 1993 that the last troops left. In the Baltic republics, meanwhile, as many as one in ten residents was a Soviet soldier or family member; though not all were Russian, of course, the problem ultimately became an ethnic one, as tens of thousands of retired officers claimed residency and stayed on after their troops had left (mostly by the mid-1990s).

The troop withdrawal reminds us how physical was the Soviet presence in Eastern Europe. The vast bases, cloaked in secrecy, had been symbols of Soviet domination and Soviet paranoia; as departing troops stripped them even of doors, windows, plumbing, and electrical wiring, the buildings stood as reminders of the gross plundering of resources that the communist economic system had become. East Europeans felt mostly relief as the last soldiers departed; that experience would shape their emerging alliance with the West, though in unexpected ways.

Could Eastern Europe, after half a century of communist rule, belong to any alliance at all? Neutrality, after all, had been one of the watchwords of Hungary's 1956 and of the Prague Spring. Certainly no one lamented the demise of the Warsaw Pact, the unequal alliance that had served to justify Soviet domination since 1955. The Pact folded with a whimper in July, 1991; this moment was probably the apogee of belief that the end of the Cold War would usher in a new era of non-alignment or multipolarity. As Václav Havel put it in his much-applauded speech to a joint session of the United States Congress in February 1990: "these revolutionary changes will enable us to escape from the rather antiquated straitjacket of this bipolar view of the world, and to enter at last into an era of multipolarity."[4] But already, events were unfolding that would convince both East and West Europeans to embrace military alliances as a solution to the problems of the European continent.

The first such event was the show of Soviet force in the Baltics in January 1991. Timothy Snyder has captured the dramatic revision of Polish thinking at that time. As Polish diplomats returned home from an old-fashioned Soviet harangue on why Poland should be grateful that Soviet troops still remained in their country, their plane was diverted from a planned refueling in Vilnius. "They could see the reason from their [airplane] windows," Snyder writes. "Vilnius was aflame, under attack from Soviet special forces."[5] Nor did the threat fade when the troops left and the Soviet Union disintegrated. In 2002, during negotiations over Russian access to its Kaliningrad province, Russian officials demanded unrestricted access to a land corridor running across northeast Poland – exactly as Hitler had done in the months before his September 1939 invasion. The lessons from such encounters were double: first, in case anyone in Poland doubted it, the time for gratitude to the Soviet Army had long ago passed; second, the countries of Eastern Europe needed to rely on one another, more than they ever had before.

New neighbors

The first decades of independence, between the World Wars, were marred by petty differences among small, vulnerable states. Poland, Hungary, and Bulgaria, for example, did not form stable alliances with any of their neighbors; the first two of these spent much of that period plotting or carrying out invasions instead. The communist era, in contrast, imposed alliances that could hardly be called cooperative, as could be seen when all of Czechoslovakia's communist neighbors, plus Bulgaria, invaded it in 1968.

There has been, to be sure, plenty of evidence that old rivalries could still dampen post-1989 feelings of euphoria and brotherhood. The first independent regional alliance was the formation of the so-called Visegrad group, comprising Poland, Czechoslovakia, and Hungary, founded in February 1991. But while the three countries' leaders pledged to cooperate closely with one another toward integration into Europe, the honeymoon was brief. Less than two years later, Czech Prime Minister Václav Klaus, having just shed his Slovak burden, announced that Visegrad was an "artificial process" created by the West, and that the Czech Republic would journey toward Europe on its own.[6] This competition for Western graces would recur time and again, fading only as East Europeans came to see themselves more as partners, not penitents.

Minority issues have, not surprisingly, given rise to more serious international discord. Before the break-up of Yugoslavia, only two countries could boast significant neighboring irredenta: Poland and Hungary. For many Hungarians, the 1920 Treaty of Trianon's dismembering of Greater Hungary was still, seventy years later, hard to accept; they looked for ways to at least symbolically recover empire. Hence Prime Minister József Antall's appeal to the support of Hungarians living across the border – a tactic that would later be echoed by Franjo Tudjman and Slobodan Milošević. When Fidesz inherited the mantle of mainstream nationalism and won the election of 1998, its leader, Viktor Orbán, quickly revived the idea that Budapest could, and had the duty to, speak for its neighbors' citizens. In June 2001, Parliament overwhelmingly – with the votes of even the Socialist Party joining the nationalist right – passed the Status Law, which extended rights (short of citizenship) and access to Hungary-funded social benefits to Hungarians living in the near abroad. Interestingly, Hungarians in Austria were excepted from the law, as its discriminatory nature rendered it invalid in the EU.

Depending on one's perspective, this was either a prelude to a Hitlerian demand for *Lebensraum*, or simply an effort to protect and promote the culture of a small nation. The socialist government elected in 2002 passed a softer version of the law, and ultimately put it to a referendum, in December 2004. By that time Hungary had joined the EU, and the pendulum had swung away from "Greater Hungary." Only 37 percent, split almost evenly, bothered to vote, making the referendum, and the law, invalid. To its neighbors, though, Hungary remains a somewhat uncertain ally.

Two countries in particular have taken the opposite tack, putting aside traditionally rancorous relations. Both Bulgaria and Poland have been guided by a kind of *Realpolitik*, as well as by a sense that aggressive nationalism was no longer a useful path to political power. Bulgaria had managed to be on the aggressor and losing side of three wars in a row during the twentieth century; additionally, minority issues soured its relationship with Turkey and with Macedonia. The realization that Bulgaria had fallen behind its neighbors in terms of economic and political change provoked huge demonstrations, early elections, and a change of government in 1997, in which the center-right Union of Democratic Forces ousted the socialists. The old government had followed the Zhivkov tradition in exploiting Bulgarian nationalism; the new government thus pursued Europe instead. Improved recognition of the rights of the Turkish and Bulgarian Muslim minorities led to trade and military agreements with Turkey. Greece became an ally in Bulgaria's quest for NATO membership. Most important, Bulgaria ended in 1999 its objection to the existence of a separate Macedonian language and nation.

Poland's transformation was equally dramatic. Like Bulgarians, Poles were not used to seeing their neighbors as allies instead of threats. But the events of 1989 had given Poles a sense of being leaders in the region. Thus as Lithuania, Belarus, and Ukraine moved toward independence, their Polish minorities did not become objects of desire, but a reason for Poland to become a patron of nascent democracies. The Polish minority in Lithuania was particularly vocal in demanding political autonomy; yet, Poland's political leaders thoroughly rebuffed its overtures. Polish opinion came to see the Lithuanian Poles not, primarily, as victims needing Poland's protection (though of course such proposals surfaced), but as communist holdovers endangering Lithuanian democracy. Lithuanian fears of Polish culture were a stronger obstacle, but by 1997, Lithuania and Poland had become close allies.

Lithuanians might still resent Poland's regional power aspirations; among Western-oriented Ukrainians (an ever-increasing faction), the attitude is rather different. During the 1990s, they realized that independence did not equal "freedom"; a visitor from Poland would be pestered for comparisons: could Ukraine follow Poland's path? Poland (with fewer citizens, but a larger economy) was a model for Ukrainian nationalists. As one put it in 1990: "We know that the path to Europe ... really does lead through Poland."[7] Poland became the main advocate of Ukraine's interests to Western Europe. The events of 2004 showed just how far Polish–Ukrainian relations had come: a transformation at least as impressive as the French–German rapprochement of the 1950s. First, the two countries' parliaments painstakingly hammered out a resolution commemorating the tragic ethnic cleansing of Polish–Ukrainian borderlands during and after World War Two, in which tens of thousands were killed, and hundreds of thousands forcibly relocated. The debates were painful and sometimes acrimonious, but ended with a reconciliation ceremony on the sixtieth anniversary in June 2003. Polish good-will toward Ukraine reached its height during Ukraine's December 2004 Orange Revolution. Wearing orange became almost obligatory in Warsaw, and thousands of young Poles, eager to experience what their parents had in 1980 or 1989, traveled to Kyiv to cheer at demonstrations and monitor the elections.

NATO expands

Both Poland and Ukraine would be rewarded for their international efforts, becoming partners in another international alliance dominated by a superpower. For this to happen, it was necessary not only that Western, and particularly American, interest in the region (and in points further east, of course) increase. Eastern Europeans were the first to understand the dangers that post-communist nationalism posed to international stability. It would take many years, and several wars, before the West came to understand this as well.

Many of the early arguments for NATO expansion were quite symbolic: that the wrongs of the Cold War needed to be righted; that one could no longer speak of a "European security" that excluded so many; that Russia needed to be reminded just who had won the face-off between communism and democracy. Arguments against tended to be rather more concrete: the expansion of NATO could not be shown to increase international stability, nor to promote democracy, especially since the latter had never been a requirement for membership. It would not obviously contain Russia, and indeed could have the opposite effect, by provoking Russia into reclaiming control over countries left between NATO and itself. As British Home Secretary Michael Howard put it: "placing Central Europe on the front line of a new confrontation is an odd way to ensure its security."[8] Finally, some, like US Secretary of Defense Les Aspin, argued that an expanded NATO would simply replicate the Cold War: "We spent two generations trying to lift the Iron Curtain. We don't want to replace it by drawing another line."[9] Of course, this dodged the question of whether, if no expansion took place, NATO's border would not remain an Iron one.

The negotiations over German unification in 1990 in fact suggested that some other form of international alliance for the new democracies might emerge. In the so-called 2+4 discussions – that is, the two German states plus their erstwhile occupiers, the four victorious allies from World War Two – the NATO membership of a unified Germany was one of the more difficult issues. It was one thing to see East Germany disappear, but could it simply be thrown from the Warsaw Pact into the opposing camp? Mikhail Gorbachev proposed German neutrality, or even simultaneous membership in NATO and the Warsaw Pact. Negotiators cast about for other international bodies – the Conference on Security and Cooperation in Europe, the obscure Western European Union – that might somehow ameliorate the impression of Soviet-bloc capitulation. Given this caution, Eastern Europe – even Poland, which repeatedly sought a place at the 2+4 table (because of lingering uncertainties over how German unification would impact the new state's border with Poland) – simply could not even be part of the discussion. Western leaders hoped that Eastern Europe would find its own solution. Perhaps it would form its own security alliance, or reshape the Warsaw Pact into a more equal relationship, or choose an Austrian-style neutrality.[10]

By 1997, NATO was ready to open negotiations toward membership with three Central European countries, Poland, the Czech Republic, and Hungary, all of which joined in April 1999. Broadly, four factors led to this change in favor of expansion. The first of these has already been discussed: continued concern about Russian intentions led East Europeans to insist that a Europe without blocs (that is, stable military alliances) was not really a good thing. Second, domestic American concerns played a role. Perhaps NATO would not have grown so soon had not President Bill Clinton been thinking of his place in history after his 1996 reelection, and thus been tempted to make a bold move. Within the East European context, two often-overlooked factors are particularly worthy of attention here: first, the Yugoslav wars both increased American appreciation of the importance of the region while showing that some countries could be valuable strategic partners. Second, it became clear that the European Union was nowhere near ready to offer any East European countries membership. The costs and strictures of NATO membership being rather lower, it emerged as an acceptable consolation prize. It helped that two of the principal shapers of American foreign policy in the 1990s, Madeleine Albright (Ambassador to the United Nations, then Secretary of State) and Richard Holbrooke (Assistant Secretary of State, then Ambassador to the UN), both had strong East European ties: Albright through her Czech–Jewish heritage, and Holbrooke as principal US negotiator during the Yugoslav crises.

The mysteries of Yugoslavia

Western military powers – NATO, the EU, and the United Nations – utterly misread and mishandled the wars in Yugoslavia, and contributed directly both to its disintegration and to the ethnic cleansing and genocide that followed. It may therefore seem odd to link that débâcle to the eventual expansion of NATO and the EU. It would also be folly to assert that those expansions have put an end to international or domestic conflicts among the new member-states. However, the contrast between the approach to the Yugoslav crises and the ultimate integration of the region does suggest that Europe and the West embarked in 1991 on a steep learning curve, discovering just how different the post-Cold War world would be from the old one.

From the very first signs of imminent conflict between Belgrade and the republics of Slovenia and Croatia Western leaders thought this crisis was one that Europe should be able to handle. The United States had just led a victorious coalition against Iraq in the Gulf War, and the Middle East would continue to be the major American preoccupation. US Secretary of State James Baker visited Belgrade days before Slovenia and Croatia declared independence in June 1991; he offered no support for secession, and appeared to be grasping for ways to preserve Yugoslavia.[11] The United States had little interest in Yugoslavia; after all, German unification had meant the formal withdrawal of American supervision (as opposed to American presence, of course) from the European continent. The European Community, by contrast, saw the Yugoslav conflict as an ideal test of its integration. As the superpowers withdrew from the Cold War arena, could not Europe emerge as a world power, with diplomatic reach to match its economic strength? As Luxembourg's Foreign Minister Jacques Poos famously declared: "The hour of Europe has dawned."[12]

What could "Europe" do? By June 1991, Yugoslavia (at least with Milošević's hand on the steering wheel) was doomed. Political and economic strains had rendered it untenable. Yet as noted in Chapter 2, outsiders persisted in seeing only ethnic conflict. European negotiators who arrived in Yugoslavia to find a way out of the Slovene war were trapped by the ideas of national self-determination that Woodrow Wilson had brought to Paris seventy-one years before. From the plebiscites that then accompanied the carving up of fallen empires, through the population transfers approved at Potsdam in

1945, Western leaders had accepted the axiom that proper drawing of borders, accompanied if necessary by the unmixing (to use a euphemism) of populations, could assure both democracy and stability. There are a great many rights more important than to be governed by leaders of the same culture or ethnicity, but the principle of self-determination came to be regarded as the foundation of all else.

The ghost of Wilson was surely present on the Yugoslav island of Brioni in the summer of 1991, as EC leaders sought to resolve the first Yugoslav conflict. Especially since Milošević had lost interest in Serb-less Slovenia, the northernmost republic appeared to be an easy problem to resolve alone. Not that the Brioni Accord actually resolved anything: it merely called for the deactivation of Slovene and Yugoslav Army forces and the postponement of steps relating to independence, and gave Slovenia control of its borders. But some European countries – led by Latvia and Lithuania, among others – recognized Slovenia within days, with Germany in particular pushing for European recognition (which came in December 1991).[13] The effect was both to open the road for further dismemberment of Yugoslavia, and to affirm the value of an ethnically homogeneous territory.

Having opened a Pandora's box, the EC now attempted to rectify its haste. It created the Badinter Commission (led by French judge Robert Badinter) to identify preconditions to be met by seceding republics seeking international recognition. Yet the plot thickened: though only Slovenia and Macedonia thus qualified for recognition, Germany in any case upstaged the Commission by recognizing Croatia as well. Europe's resolution of the Slovene War had identified ethnic cohesion as a mark of an independent state; at the same time, recognition of Croatia, which did not even control fully its own territory, had the effect of postponing the resolution of ethnic questions. Europe's confused signals facilitated Franjo Tudjman's cleansing – symbolic, then military – of Croatia; forced multi-ethnic Bosnia into the realization that secession was the only possible (if questionable) road to survival; and made Milošević's drive for a Greater Serbia no less logical than Hitler's quest for the Czechoslovak Sudetenland.

Mercifully perhaps, the European Union (as the Community became after January 1, 1993) now gave up trying to resolve the Yugoslav problem. The torch – not so much an Olympic flame as an arsonist's weapon – passed now to the United Nations. In this phase, the Croatian War would draw the rest of Eastern Europe on to the international stage. From the time the Yugoslav Army invaded Eastern Slavonia, Tudjman had called for United Nations peacekeepers. Eventually, Milošević agreed, and UNPROFOR (United Nations Protection Force) came into being. The first of some 38,000 troops from more than thirty countries deployed across Croatia in March 1992. Just a few months later, UNPROFOR was extended to the Bosnian conflict as well. While the largest contributors to the force were France and Great Britain, both Czechoslovakia and Poland contributed over a thousand troops each. As Ronald Asmus notes: "few things more vividly demonstrated how NATO could transcend past Cold War divisions" than the close cooperation of troops once on opposite sides of the Iron Curtain.[14]

Eastern Europe was drawn into the fray in other ways as well. First, of course, the war was uncomfortably nearby: Hungary, Romania, Bulgaria, and Albania all bordered Yugoslavia; Hungary and Albania both had significant minorities within Serbia (and smaller ones in other republics). Second, the war exposed quite clearly the profound contradictions in Western relations with Eastern Europe. While some – like Slovene Foreign Minister Dimitrij Rupel, who took pains to separate his country from the "Balkans"[15] – tried to suggest that Yugoslavia was in another part of the world, it was not hard to wonder whether the belief in "ancient ethnic hatreds" might someday be applied to other Eastern conflicts. Finally, dissidents who had fought for human rights against communist dictatorships recognized a familiar cause, and a duty to fight injustice suffered by a neighbor. In 1992, Tadeusz Mazowiecki, the former prime minister of Poland, was appointed Special Rapporteur for Yugoslavia to the UN Human Rights Commission. He would resign in 1995, in protest over Western inaction at Srebrenica; in 1998, he was succeeded by Jiří Dienstbier, former Foreign Minister of Czechoslovakia.

What did the West really understand about Yugoslavia in the crucial years 1992–95? A lot less than did Yugoslavia's neighbors, for sure. Balkan specialists cringed to hear what book President Clinton had on his bedside table in 1993. Robert Kaplan's best-selling *Balkan Ghosts* gave Clinton a picture of people chained to the past, constantly reopening old wounds in search of revenge. Warren Christopher's lament that Bosnia was simply a "problem from hell" echoed British Prime Minister Neville Chamberlain's claim, in 1938, that Czechoslovakia was "a faraway country about which we know nothing."[16]

The alternative to this hand-washing was to divide the people of Bosnia so that their supposedly natural proclivities would be denied. This was the idea behind the Vance–Owen Plan (drawn up by Britain's Lord David Owen and former US Secretary of State Cyrus Vance) of 1993: to carve up Bosnia into ten cantons, each with a specific ethnic profile – three Serb, three Muslim, two Croat, one Croat-Muslim, and one, Sarajevo, shared by all three. A central government would have minimal power, most of that devolving to the ethnic cantons. A charitable view would be that not only was true reconstitution of Bosnia in all its multi-ethnic complexity impossible, but cantonization might also force ethnic communities, too small to govern on their own, to cooperate with one another. Yet the Vance–Owen plan would not only render irreversible a year's worth of ethnic cleansing (Serbs would have to give up some acquired land to Bosnian Muslims, but both they and the Croats would hold land from which they had expelled so many), but would also seem to dictate further cleansing: *cuius regio, eius religio* would be the motto, and since ideology had made ethnic conversion impossible, those who were different would have to leave. The plan ultimately failed, though aspects of it survived in later negotiations.

As any East European could recognize, Western policy toward Yugoslavia reflected its policy toward the region as a whole. The end of the Cold War now confronted military powers with conflicts that lacked any evident security interest. As in Somalia and Haiti at the same time, the West floundered for a cause as compelling as the old battle of ideologies. Metaphors of backwardness and decrepitude colored Western discourse about Eastern Europe whether the topic was ethnic cleansing or foreign aid. East Europeans were expected to pull themselves up out of their isolation in order to show themselves

worthy of assistance. The West merely imposed rules and requirements, and appeared to reward aggressors and *faits accomplis*: communist nomenklatura who had become bosses of industry; Russian
generals who jealously guarded their old sphere of influence; Serb
ethnic cleansers. Western policy toward the region until 1997–98
was half-hearted and distant, full of empty gestures.

The United Nations forces, in turn, engendered decidedly mixed
feelings. "Peacekeeping" had turned out to mean enforcing the
gains of the victors and preventing those attacked, generally the
Bosnian Muslims, from defending themselves. When, for example,
UNPROFOR troops deployed to Srebrenica in 1993 collected Bosnian
weapons as part of an agreement, leaving the surrounding Bosnian
Serb Army fully armed, were the interests of peace really advanced?
Humanitarian aid had certainly saved the lives of tens of thousands
of refugees, but it meant, too, acquiescence to ethnic cleansing.
Refugees left their homes in UN buses, while others found themselves trapped in UN "safe areas." "We're becoming collaborators,"
one UN aid worker told Laura Silber and Alan Little in July 1992.
"The choice we face is either to become agents of ethnic cleansing,
or to leave tens of thousands of people to continue living their night-
mare."[17] In the last year of their presence, peacekeepers had even
become hostages. The images of UN soldiers chained to lampposts
or fences at Serb military installations to prevent their bombing
exemplified the helplessness – or the indifference, depending on
one's level of rancor – of the UN forces.

The UN, however, does not deserve to shoulder all the scorn and
ridicule alone – and there is plenty to go around. The UNPROFOR
agreement specified that NATO forces, stationed in Italy, provided
backup firepower as necessary. NATO planes enforced the no-fly
zone imposed on Bosnia. In practice, NATO presence meant very
little. In one small but telling fiasco, the two forces were unable
even to eliminate a single Serb anti-aircraft weapon on Mt. Igman,
endangering all flights in and out of Sarajevo.[18]

The genocide carried out in Srebrenica in July 1995, and a particularly horrific shelling of a Sarajevo square in August, finally broke the
pattern. Serb atrocities had become obvious enough that the fighting
had to be stopped – though a Bosnian Army offensive later that

summer, which threatened to upend the ethnic balance envisioned by the West, also spurred intervention. First, NATO carried out a two-week bombing of Bosnian Serb targets. Then, the Americans summoned all parties to the Dayton talks, at which the Bosnian war came to an end. The agreements at Dayton ushered in a new, third phase of international involvement, as NATO, through a new force called IFOR (Implementation Force), took over from UNPROFOR. Dayton did not, of course, really terminate the conflict; too many loose ends remained. Bosnia was neither divided nor restored: instead, it became two separate entities, the Serb Republic and the Muslim–Croat Federation, joined loosely by a central government. But by bringing some 60,000 NATO troops formally into the heart of the former Yugoslavia, it may have, however awkwardly and indirectly, helped to bring the end into distant view.

IFOR's mandate expired after Bosnia's first election in late 1996; the new Stabilization Force (SFOR), with about 32,000 troops, also predominantly from NATO members, succeeded it as the mission changed from implementing the Dayton Agreement to maintaining it. The main duties of the troops were to keep the former warring sides apart; to ensure the functioning of local government; to assist in the return of refugees (for many host nations in Western Europe, this was the most ardently desired outcome of the settlement); and to apprehend war criminals. For the first several years at least, success in these last two areas was minimal. Three years after the war, only about 15 percent of those who had left Bosnia entirely had returned; nearly all of these were directed into ethnic enclaves, not necessarily home. The focus slowly shifted to helping refugees recover their homes. Often, though, busloads of returnees under SFOR escort were turned back by crowds of rock-throwing Serbs. The authority set up to adjudicate claims on prewar property had processed nearly a quarter-million claims through 2002, much of the repossession was only on paper.[19] The balance sheet in the hunt for war criminals in Bosnia is similarly mixed. Thus Radovan Karadzić has been able to elude capture for ten years, because SFOR and Western politicians have been reluctant to risk soldiers. Searches were rare, in fact, until 2002; one well-known raid in that year was said to have failed because a French officer tipped off the Bosnian Serb police.

Nation-building in NATO and the EU

In earlier chapters, we saw that the Yugoslav wars were a crucial moment in the history of European nationalism, in the understanding and treatment of war crimes, and in the development of Balkan politics. They also transformed the relationship between the whole of Eastern Europe and the West from one of dependence to one more symbiotic. Perhaps it is a paradox, but the Yugoslav wars, rather than thrusting Eastern Europe to the periphery, helped Western powers understand how much the security of Europe depended on deeper cooperation. Half-measures, like the Partnership for Peace created in 1994 for all interested post-Soviet (or neutral) countries, could not suffice. Poland, the largest country in the region, the one (apart from the Baltics) most threatened by Russia, and the one most celebrated in the West for its defeat of communism, reproached its Western allies most vocally. By the time of the Dayton Agreements, Eastern Europe had become a key player in the Yugoslav drama. The military base at Taszár, in southern Hungary near the (Serb) Yugoslav border, became a staging ground for NATO troops in December 1995. Eastern European countries contributing to IFOR clearly saw it as an important step toward a closer alliance. Polish forces, for example, chose to serve under American command in Tuzla, Bosnia.

In the winter of 1996–97, the vague promise of NATO expansion swiftly acquired a concrete schedule. President Clinton's Republican opponents had made NATO expansion – and the drawdown of American troops in Bosnia – a campaign issue; determined to seize the initiative, Clinton set 1999 as the deadline for admission. Over the previous few years, Poland, the Czech Republic, and Hungary had shown that they were most capable of integrating into NATO with a minimum of difficulty, and that their political systems were sufficiently democratic to satisfy skeptics. The three received invitations at a NATO summit in Madrid in July 1997, and formally joined in April 1999, as part of the celebration of the alliance's fiftieth anniversary. In 2004, the Baltic countries, Slovakia, Bulgaria, Romania, and Slovenia also joined.

Ironically perhaps, the expansion took place just as the alliance was embarking on its first formal military action, in Kosovo. We can leave aside farfetched explanations – such as the protection of non-existent oil pipelines, or that Kosovo is somehow the vital cross-roads of southeastern Europe; the war with Milošević's Yugoslavia over Kosovo happened because NATO powers (most importantly the United States, although with the nascent East European members, among others, also weighing in) realized that the delayed response in Bosnia had been a colossal error. Instead of pacifying Milošević, they had encouraged him. Support of Tudjman, too, had led to war crimes too obvious to ignore. Vague support for the multi-ethnic traditions of the region had ended up condoning ethnic cleansing. The conjunction with the fiftieth anniversary commemorations of the Holocaust, the ritual invocation and desecration of the "Never Again" pledge – for example at the opening of the United States Holocaust Memorial Museum, in 1993 – and the presence in power of leaders, like United States Secretary of State Madeleine Albright, to whom preventing genocide had become a matter of policy, moved the foreign policy needle ever so briefly toward the moral side of the gauge.

Accusations that the world overreacted in Kosovo, wreaking havoc unnecessarily, can never be fully resolved. The heart of this argument is that, when Albright dragged Milošević to the negotiating table at Rambouillet in March 1999, seeking to make up for the neglect of the Kosovo problem at Dayton three-and-a-half years earlier, she devised a trap. The non-negotiable terms offered Milošević included extensive autonomy for Kosovo within Yugoslavia, with its own government and a large peacekeeping force. There was also a vague promise of further steps, probably toward independence, to be taken after three years. Serbia would control the region in name only. All in all, this was an offer Milošević had to refuse. It is equally clear, however, that, after three wars, there was no sense in repeating the patterns of previous diplomacy: extensive negotiation would simply enable further ethnic cleansing, and Milošević would find a way to deny any involvement. While this meant that Rambouillet was based as much on previous betrayals as on present realities, the prospect of another round of ethnic cleansing provoked Albright to try a preemptive approach.

The conduct of the war itself, though, raises another question: If the cause was moral, was it worth the risk of soldiers' lives? President

Clinton decided otherwise, and took the possibility of a land invasion off the table even before the war began. As a result, the campaign consisted entirely of bombing runs at high altitude over Kosovo and Serbia proper. Some 500 civilians died, some as the result of attacks on non-military targets;[20] the Serbian regime, meanwhile, took advantage of the absence of enemy troops to initiate a massive ethnic-cleansing program. That the Kosovo war achieved its main aims – the prevention of genocide and, eventually, the end of the Milošević regime – has had the unfortunate consequence of setting an example of how to change bad regimes. The attempt at remote-control nation-building in the Middle East since 2003 is directly a product of the Kosovo experience.

The real error at Rambouillet, meanwhile, was not the treatment of Serbia, but the willingness to overlook the dangers posed by radicalism among Kosovar Albanians. As the indictment of Kosovar Prime Minister Harudinaj shows, it is still not certain whether the KLA can be a force for stability, or whether the war succeeded in stopping genocide only to encourage a reverse ethnic cleansing. NATO's victory, in June 1999, brought an occupation force, KFOR, which, along with a UN peacekeeping force, UNMIK, has embarked on the most extensive program of Western nation-building in the region. In a way, Kosovo is a test case for the ability of Western intervention, armed and otherwise, to change the face of Eastern Europe. In essence, the goal has been to make Kosovo, if its citizens wish to gain statehood, as much like the rest of the region as possible.

If that is so, it is worth considering for a moment what the model to follow might be. The discourse of the last two decades has been dominated by the concept of the "open society," George Soros's program of building democracy through support of independent media, education, and electoral processes. Soros's Central European University in Budapest has advanced a discourse of civil rights and democratic change, training thousands of students from around the region. At another level, he has contributed tens of millions of dollars to stabilizing democracy, in Macedonia for example.[21] Not only have Western NGOs (and governments) followed through on this program everywhere, but East Europeans themselves have pushed for the same freedoms.

If, however, one examines the entire region in search of countries where democracy has been the most successful: where extremism appears to be marginal, civil rights of citizens are least threatened, and civil society flourishes, and where electoral turnover occurs without violent resistance – then one returns over and over to the same cases: Slovenia, Poland, Hungary, perhaps the Czech Republic. All are largely homo-ethnic, and in this are unlike their neighbors. Turning one's gaze to Kosovo (or Bosnia, or Croatia), one can then ask: Does expulsion of minorities make democracy easier? Has the West, while praising the virtues of multi-ethnicity, and urging East Europeans to save that part of local traditions, helped to create societies that thrive by honoring multi-ethnicity only as a tradition and not as an actual practice?

It is not at all clear that multi-ethnicity – especially if it conflicts with democracy or stability – is the most desired or valuable feature of modern society. If it is, though, then the supra-national European Union is one of its best guarantors. While there is no lack of national tension in Western Europe, the Union has also given minorities an ally above the state. Thinking in these terms, one could argue that the best way to avoid the Yugoslav wars would have been to offer Yugoslavia (the whole thing, all six republics) in 1989 a concrete timetable for near-term entry into the European Community. Malcolm Chalmers has calculated the price of war and peace in Yugoslavia, estimating costs to the international community (not including Yugoslavia's East European neighbors) of peacekeeping, military intervention, humanitarian assistance, and reconstruction to be 107 billion dollars. A comprehensive package of debt relief and development assistance, in contrast, would have come to approximately 11 billion.[22] Accelerated admission to the Union would thus have been both cost-effective and humanitarian, saving the lives of at least 120,000 people.

So much for "what-ifs." Through the early 1990s, the European Union was even more reluctant to open itself to new members than was NATO. The arguments for accepting new members from Eastern Europe were strong: Spain, Portugal, and Greece had started on the path to membership not long after ridding themselves of dictatorships in the 1970s, despite their relative poverty. Greece, in turn, was really the only member (until Finland joined in 1995) that allowed the organization to call itself "European," without the adjective "Western." From the very beginning, proponents of the European Community invoked European values and European heritage; why, then, keep Eastern Europe at arm's length, especially when the revolutions of 1989 had centered on the pursuit of European political and economic opportunities?

Poland, Hungary, and Czechoslovakia signed association agreements with the EC in December 1991; these agreements contained no specific promises, but acknowledged that accession to membership was "the ultimate aim" of the three supplicants.[23] For the next several years, Western European leaders refused even to discuss a timetable for negotiations (let alone for actual accession). The principal cause for hesitation, usually stated somewhat indirectly, was that the newly-opened markets of the East could not withstand free competition with vigorous Western economies. Thus, immediate accession would both place a significant burden on the West (which would have to subsidize its eastern neighbors heavily), while destroying support for nascent economic reform in the East. There were two obvious problems with this argument. First, the logic of the Community, from its beginnings in French–German rapprochement, had always been that close economic cooperation would vitiate political tensions, and thus avoid a return to perennial conflict on the continent. Surely, it was therefore imperative to breach the Iron Curtain as quickly and decisively as possible, using economic partnership to erase any vestige of antagonism. Secondly, concerns about Eastern Europe's economic competitiveness sometimes masked opposite concerns: that cheap labor, as well as inexpensive food and other exports, would flood Western markets. Who, then, was unprepared for competition, East or West? Indeed, various forms of Western protectionism have accompanied every step of the accession process. Even today, when eight Eastern European countries are already members, many older members of the European Union seem most to fear competition from Eastern workers and goods.

This is not to say that the European Union did not make an effort to assist its Eastern neighbors. In fall 1989, even before the revolutions were over, the European Community created PHARE (Polish and Hungarian Assistance for the Reconstruction of Europe), an aid program later extended across the region. Most of this aid – the program concluded in 2005, dispensing around a billion dollars annually – went toward financial restructuring, encouragement of private enterprise, and infrastructure development. The European Bank for Reconstruction and Development (EBRD), created in 1991, disperses loans that also aim at economic transformation. One should not forget many much smaller projects. The Scandinavian countries, for example, have funded smokestack scrubbers and sewage-treatment plants in Poland and the Baltic states, in an effort to improve their own environment as well.

Critics of the EBRD in particular are legion. Especially in its early days, the EBRD was famed for spending as much on lavish parties and opulent offices as on actual aid. More importantly, both the EBRD and PHARE – like the International Monetary Fund or the World Bank, for that matter – come with strings attached. There is more than one definition of private enterprise, and more than one perspective on the proper role of the state in the economy, after all. Recipient countries have questioned, for example, the apparent preference for support of foreign-investment ventures over domestic initiatives, and for large industry over small enterprises. And the EBRD's requirement that projects be financially viable and able to repay loans at relatively high rates drew this retort from Vladimír Dlouhý, Czech Minister of Trade and Industry, in 1993: "It is difficult to make a distinction between the EBRD and the commercial banks. There must be a difference, because if there isn't, then why in God's name did we set it up?"[24]

The problems with economic assistance only highlighted the need to move more quickly toward EU membership. But the difficulties in admitting new post-communist members also had political roots. In the early 1990s, the European Community was itself in the midst of a transformation. Economic cooperation, with all of its squabbles over subsidies and market access, proved to be simple compared to social or political coordination in the European Union. Some members envisaged something approaching a United States of Europe, in which matters of social, justice, or foreign policy would be handled at the supra-state level. Others fought hard against any increase in the power of European institutions. These complicated internal struggles distracted West European leaders from what one could argue was the more important task of enlargement. Indeed, attention to eastern expansion improved after the Maastricht Treaty was ratified in 1992. The treaty achieved several important goals, including the creation of a common currency, and thus cleared the way for expansion.

At the same time, though, eastern expansion placed political questions squarely in the center. That is, the question of admitting a large number of post-communist democratizing countries naturally encouraged rhetoric about political requirements – an issue avoided when the former dictatorships of Southern Europe had been admitted in the 1980s. Thus European Union leaders instructed prospective members in June 1993 that "membership requires that the candidate country has achieved stability of institutions guaranteeing democracy, the rule of law, human rights and respect for and protection of minorities."[25] The point is not that this was a higher standard than that asked of previous prospective members; though, after Maastricht, that was true. Rather, this enlargement process, perhaps unavoidably, brought rhetoric about the moral–political nature of Europeanness from the abstract into the concrete. Quite unexpectedly, the Eastern enlargement would force East Europeans – and West Europeans, too – to reconsider what Europe meant.

In the meantime, East European countries advanced increasingly strident demands for concrete timetables. Hungary and Poland were the first to apply for membership, in 1994; within two years, the rest of the region (except Albania and the former Yugoslav countries beyond Slovenia) had also applied. The stirrings of NATO expansion, and the Yugoslav wars, also had their effect, as did the fact that by the mid-1990s the economies of the non-Balkan East European countries were experiencing a boom, and no longer looked like potential millstones around Europe's neck. At its July 1997 meeting in Brussels, the European Commission (the EU's main administrative body) judged six applicants (Poland, Hungary, the Czech Republic, Slovenia, and Estonia, as well as Cyprus) to be ready to begin negotiations toward membership. EU leaders accepted the recommendations that December, and negotiations began late the following year. Intense lobbying on behalf of the other two Baltic countries, and the fall of Mečiar in Slovakia, led to those countries joining negotiations in 2000.

The actual negotiation process, which was subdivided into discussion of thirty separate chapters of the common laws of the European Union – the *acquis communautaire* – was a triumph of bureaucracy over politics. Mind-numbing coordination of everything from agricultural policy to statistical formats to environmental standards replaced the hand-wringing over general political preparedness. Now, the member countries focused on exacting acceptable prices (such as barriers to Western labor markets) for admission. East European publics, in turn, followed the artificial race to close as many of the chapter negotiations as quickly as possible, worrying less about details than about deadlines.

The greatest anxieties were not necessarily the most rational ones. In the fight over mutual access to labor markets and property, for example, Eastern Europe was forced to accept transition periods of up to seven years, during which citizens of newly-admitted countries would not be able to move freely to the West in search of work. Just three countries, Great Britain, Sweden and Ireland, did not impose such restrictions; in 2005, labor shortages in others (such as Spain and Greece) prompted reconsideration of the ban. In May, the specter of "Polish plumbers" who would take work away from their French counterparts became a symbol of the failure of a French referendum on the European constitution; Poland's travel agency responded with ads showing a muscular model in overalls, clutching a plumber's wrench and sporting a smoldering gaze, under the slogan: "I'm staying in Poland. Come visit!"

Agriculture seems to produce the most fears; indeed, it haunts nearly every EU discussion about money. The "old" member countries worried that cheaper foodstuffs would flood their markets and deprive their farmers of livelihood. The prospective members pointed out that the hefty agricultural subsidies to wealthier member-states (especially France) put Eastern farmers at a distinct disadvantage. They demanded equal subsidies and equal market access – and generally got neither (though results varied in the separate negotiations). The budget difficulties that haunted the EU for at least the previous twenty years have thus been frozen into place: instead of a phase-out of agricultural subsidies (one of the principal demands that Britain especially has made on Europe), those subsidies have become a sacred cow in the cult of Europe, and threatening to the East–West relationship.

As during the approach to NATO, the negotiations with the EU prompted a new set of anxieties in Eastern Europe, about loss of sovereignty and resubjugation to a far-away bureaucracy of central planning. On the one hand were Thatcherite free marketeers and libertarians – most prominently Václav Klaus, the erstwhile Czech prime minister, elected president in 2003. On the other, extreme nationalist or populist parties, which stirred fears of invasion by foreign bankers and imposition of alien cultural practices (euthanasia, for example, or gay marriage). Critical, then, was the surprisingly reassuring voice of the Vatican. In his visits to communist Poland (he was unable to visit other East European countries until after 1989), Pope John Paul II had conveyed a message crucial to the success of anti-communist opposition in his homeland: "Be not afraid." He repeated this message in the context of European integration as well, during visits to Croatia, Poland, and other candidate countries. On a pilgrimage to Greece in 2001, the Pope and Archbishop Christopoulos, head of the Orthodox Church of Greece, issued a statement "rejoic[ing] at the success and progress of the European Union. The union of the European world in one civil entity, without her people losing their national self-awareness, traditions, and identity, has been the vision of its pioneers."[26] Though differences would emerge in subsequent debates on the European Constitution, the assumption conveyed here was that Eastern Europe would strengthen Europe, and not be itself weakened or threatened by the Union.

The EU summit in Copenhagen in December 2002, at which ten countries (eight from Eastern Europe, plus Malta and Cyprus) were formally invited to join, ushered in a year of ratification by both members and candidates, and some nail-biting. Most of the post-communist candidates chose to put the matter to a referendum, and in some cases polls predicted a relatively close vote. In the end, the vote was everywhere decisively in favor, ranging from 67 percent in Estonia and Latvia to 92 percent in Slovakia. Anxieties about the surrender of sovereignty proved less important than the sense that there was only one way to be part of Europe, and only one way to have access to the goods and jobs that the richer part of the continent might have to offer. In addition, the EU was already ubiquitous, as new roads and urban renewal projects across the region sported the blue-with-gold-stars emblem.

One could get the impression, especially from the national media, that the EU was simply a source of cash, measured in the billions of euros, whose generosity would only increase. The fabled EU bureaucracy was a more complicated matter: when EU inspectors (well before accession) began certifying East European dairies or slaughterhouses for sanitary standards, hundreds of small and medium-sized firms were forced to invest in improvements or face loss of access to markets, or even closure. This was a perfect example, perhaps, of the victory of faraway bureaucrats over local practice. Yet communism, with all its corner-cutting, bribes, chronic short-ages, and poor quality was less than fifteen years in the past, and many bad habits had been hard to break. It was easy to imagine that Europe, which the average consumer/traveler associated with advanced technology and efficiency, might bring about miracles.

Whose Europe?

Though no surveys explored this question, one might say that East Europeans sought, in joining the European Union, a missing piece to the revolutions of 1989. Because the revolutions had not been violent, much had not changed. The local officials, the judges and policemen, the village mayors, even the government ministers were often the same people as before – and why not? East Europeans had chosen not to follow the path of previous revolutions, in which any association with the old regime was a serious taint on one's biography. The challenge, then, was to change communist-era prac-tices without changing the people. A leap into Europe offered this promise. While a glance at the news from, say, Belgium or Italy will confirm that the EU is hardly a bastion of clean living and rigorous public morals, East Europeans often imagined it as a panacea for the lingering afflictions they associated with their communist past.

The May 2004 expansion of the European Union was indeed different from its predecessors; unlike Great Britain, Spain, or Sweden, the new post-communist members were not welcomed as equals, but as pupils, made to accept various limitations of membership that have given them a kind of second-class status within the Union.[27] At the same time, though, this enlargement has changed Europe in surprising ways. The new members brought with them a different understanding, and different expectations, of Europe, provoking a crisis that may yet transform the continent.

We can begin in the middle of that crisis, with the infamous "Letter of Eight." In late January, 2003 – at a point when the US-led invasion of Iraq seemed all but inevitable – the leaders of eight European countries issued an open letter (organized by prime ministers Tony Blair of Britain and José María Aznar of Spain) supporting the Iraq campaign. Among the signatories were President Václav Havel, and prime ministers Leszek Miller and Péter Medgyessy of the Czech Republic, Poland, and Hungary, respectively. The letter presented a variety of reasons for the support – in part, of course, because US President George W. Bush's justifications for the war were notably varied, as well. But the emphasis was on the defense of shared values of "democracy, individual freedom, human rights and the rule of law," casting Saddam Hussein as the enemy of these and calling upon the UN Security Council to "face up to its responsibilities," an implicit endorsement of the path to war.[28] The signatures of the three post-communist leaders drew a much harsher reaction that that of their Western co-signers. After a second letter from the so-called "Vilnius Group" of ten more mostly East European countries, French President Jacques Chirac bitterly suggested that they had shown themselves unworthy of Europe by missing "a good opportunity to keep quiet."

Soon Havel, and other prominent former dissidents, found themselves accused of having betrayed the principles they had fought for under communism. In the Berlin daily *Die Tageszeitung*, Christian Semler accused them of abandoning civil society and placing their hopes in (American) political and military power. Semler sardonically labelled Havel, Adam Michnik, and Hungarian writer György Konrad the "three wise men," who now "pose as the real intellectuals of the 'new Europe' – that Europe that wants to be on the side of the victors."[29] Indeed, had the dissidents sold out? Later that month, Adam Michnik replied, in an article entitled "We, the Traitors." He compared the invasion of Saddam Hussein's Iraq to Finland's war against Stalin's Soviet Union, or Poland's fight with Hitler. "I am one of those people," he explained, "who well remember our nations' experiences with totalitarian dictatorships ... and that is why we were able to draw the right conclusions from the lessons of September 11 2001." He affirmed his deep suspicions of American militarism, and celebrated the rights of those who would protest, but concluded: "War has been declared upon the democratic world. And we want to defend that world, whose mistakes and sins we know all too well."[30]

Michnik and Semler – and the Europes they claimed to represent – were talking past one another. To be sure, from the perspective of a few years later, Michnik was too quick to draw a connection between the terrorist attack of 2001 and Iraq, and to trust in the existence of Saddam Hussein's weapons of mass destruction. Yet whether he – or Havel, or Haraszti, or many, many others of the East European intelligentsia – was right or wrong is less interesting than the sources of this argument. Michnik makes quite clear that he is hardly uninformed. Indeed, East European publics were quite knowledgeable about the Middle East. Not only was media coverage very thorough, but many engineers, doctors, and other professionals had worked in Iraq and other Arab countries when they had been Soviet bloc allies.

Support for the invasion, then, was not born of ignorance of world affairs. How important was political realism as a factor? Was East European support really offered in expectation of material support from the Americans? Poland, Bulgaria, and Romania in particular could hope to become sites for new NATO bases that might supplant those in Germany, for example. However, NATO – under pressure from Russia – made it clear that expansion would not (at least immediately) lead to redeployment of its forces. There was much realism in the region, but it had quite different meanings in the shadow of the Cold War. Political and cultural elites – and, in Poland and Romania in particular, voters as well – are guided in part by an "Atlanticist" perspective on national and European security, in which American links balance those with nearer neighbors like Russia and Germany.[31]

Michnik's sardonic title, in which he rejects the intimation that he and his colleagues had betrayed their ideals, offers a clue to his reasoning. Behind the bluster, the argument went something like this: We know what it is to live under an authoritarian dictatorship. Having won our freedom (with the help, however intangible, of the United States), we owe something to the world. We can't take on all the bad regimes of the world, but here is one that our largest ally has in its sights. Therefore, we can and must help the people of Iraq. Perhaps our experience in fighting for democracy can be of use. And most of all, it is we who are consistent in our political position; the surprise, then (to recall the encounter with Haraszti) is Western elites' inconsistent support for nations desiring freedom.

Thus, twelve of the fifteen countries of Eastern Europe (only Croatia, Serbia, and Slovenia declined) joined the "coalition of the willing," as the Bush administration called it. Most contributed the tiniest of support to the occupation: Estonia sent some forty troops, for example. Serbia, meanwhile, caused a stir when it proposed sending to Afghanistan a police unit that had previously seen duty in the ethnic cleansing of Kosovo. By far the largest commitment was that of Poland, one of only four countries to contribute combat troops to the invasion (albeit barely two hundred soldiers; its commitment to the occupation was far larger). For its support, Poland was deputized to manage one of the four occupation zones.

By 2005, enthusiasm for the restructuring of the Arab Middle East had waned significantly. The subway bombings in Madrid in March 2004 brought international terrorism uncomfortably close; Hungary and Bulgaria subsequently began withdrawing troops. Revelations about the lack of an imminent threat from Iraq has also weakened support for the occupation. But the failures of the clumsy, tone-deaf occupation regime has particular importance for Eastern Europe. Implicit in the support for toppling a dictator, as I noted above, was the idea that East Europeans also knew something about building democracy, civil society, and a viable economy. Post-Saddam Iraq was not, of course, the same as post-communist Eastern Europe.

But whether the issue was the treatment of old-regime elites or the role of foreign capital in an emerging economy, East Europeans had some experience that may have been relevant. This view, clearly, was not shared by the American leadership. After all, the American version of the Cold War's end had Ronald Reagan, not East European activists, as the main protagonist. One could say, then, that both East Europeans and Americans saw lessons of 1989 to be applied in Iraq; the American narrative of simple liberation, gratitude, and Western control triumphed, marginalizing the East European contribution once again.

Eastern Europe has encountered similar misunderstandings as it has confronted its nearer allies in Western Europe. "Europe" has turned out to mean different things East and West, though the divergent perspectives come from the same roots. The war in Iraq gathered steam just as the expansion of the European Union was entering its final phases. On February 15, 2003, huge antiwar demonstrations took to the streets of European Union capitals from London to Athens, while in Warsaw, Budapest, and elsewhere in the east barely a few hundred turned out. When German philosopher Jürgen Habermas suggested that February 15 should be considered "the birth of a European public sphere," Polish journalist Adam Krzemiński bitterly retorted that Habermas had too quickly forgotten the public sphere that had brought down communism. "No one in the West rejoiced after the East–Central European 'Autumn of the People.' In Paris or London there was actually a great deal of embarrassed discontent arising from German unification and the feared influx of the poor to the West. Even fourteen years later, there is obviously no feeling of joy within 'core Europe' over the EU's eastward expansion."[32]

Krzemiński exaggerated greatly, but it seemed clear that Habermas's "European public sphere" did not include those who had once taken to the streets (or to typewriters) under rather more adverse conditions, yet who chose now not to protest. Each side saw the other as inspired by the basest of motives: by obeisance to George W. Bush, on the one side, and by fear of loss of affluence, on the other. It is rather too early to judge this debate, but one can observe that (non-military) security was most likely the key motivator for the decision to enlarge the EU. Given that military expenditures were not involved, that is, a larger EU should mean a larger area of social and political stability. Secondarily, the 75 million new members, as they became better off and improved their infrastructure, offered both new markets and new producers for European goods.

For Eastern Europe, security and prosperity were also central, in that order: like NATO, the EU was a structure that did not include Russia, and offered a secure space for economic growth; as noted in the introduction, a space without the borders and walls that characterized the Cold War. But the centrality of values to Eastern expectations since EU enlargement on May 1, 2004, cannot be underestimated. One measure of the meaning of Europe to its new members comes from a meeting in Brussels in June 2005, at which EU leaders tried to reach a budget agreement for the years 2007–13. Amid rising rancor over farm subsidies to France and other countries, and Britain's annual rebate, several new members of the EU offered to give up some aid that they were to receive. "Nobody," said Poland's Prime Minister Marek Belka, "will be able to say that for Poland, the European Union is just a pile of money."[33] The failed summit suggested that for the older members money was indeed more important than the intangible value of Europeanness.

Since the failure of the European constitution in spring 2005, further expansion of the EU is cast in doubt. Even the accession of Romania and Bulgaria, currently scheduled for 2007, is uncertain, while the remaining countries of the region – Croatia, Serbia-Montenegro, Bosnia-Hercegovina, Macedonia, and Albania – see their hopes receding. EU leaders speak of a "black hole" in the Balkans, soon to be surrounded by member-states. The problem is which Europe should be reaching out to the states in that hole, and thus which Europe would they be asked to join. Would it be the secure, prosperous, and defensive "Old Europe" or a "New Europe" that claims to see European civilization as a goal in itself? And if the latter – what, really, is that civilization, and how does it relate to the more mundane problems that Europe faces?

Conclusion: the edge of history

Sitting in his office at *Diena*, Riga's largest daily newspaper, my friend Pauls reflected on Latvia's success. It was the spring of 2003; accession to the European Union was just over a year away, as was NATO membership. What was left, he wondered, for a country of 1.5 million people? Everything that could reasonably be achieved by a small country in the middle of Europe had been. The Latvian people had been at the center of many of the most catastrophic events of the twentieth century, from the Russian Revolution through World War Two and the Holocaust, the camps of Stalin's Siberia, and, of course, the revolutions of 1989–91. Was Latvia, like many of the other small nations of the region, from Slovenia to Estonia, becoming a poorer cousin of, say, Luxembourg, where nothing else would ever happen?

The history of Eastern Europe has not come to an end. But parts of it seem destined now to become quiet corners of the European Union. Of course, much is still going on, even in the Luxembourgs of the East. National relations are still treacherous enough in the Baltics, where hundreds of thousands holding Soviet passports have in effect no country, and where sentiment against immigrants is quite strong. The frontline of the EU and NATO may yet prove to be a hotspot of economic or political conflict. Environmental issues ranging from Baltic fish stocks to nuclear waste will have an impact on social and economic relations. It is a telling detail, though, that the three Baltic countries have each had about ten different governments since 1991, without deleterious effect on their standards of living, their neighbors, or on anything else.

If some of the post-communist lands are becoming pleasantly uneventful tourist destinations, the same cannot be said for the region as a whole. The East European countries now in the EU or on its doorstep are collectively contributing to a new Europe, the shape of which is still unknown. As they profess to take the idea of Europe seriously, while also advocating (as in the 2003–04 debate, led by Poland, over the preamble to the European constitution) a more explicit statement of European values, it may be that Europe, in the sense of the EU project, will either take on a new shape, or lose ground to a "Europe of nations," as many on the right in particular claim to prefer. And the new members' unabashed alliance with the United States, though shaken by the failure of Iraqi reconstruction, will surely continue to shape the transatlantic relationship. Eastern Europe is also the site of some of the most lively discussions in the world about the meaning of the past. In 1989, most would have expected that Poles, Czechs, and Hungarians would spend their time polishing the monuments of old, proclaiming their ancient heritage, and mugging those who disagreed. Instead, the problems of World War Two, the communist era, and 1989 itself have become important elements of national and international politics. History, in every sense, is far from over here, and there are lessons for other nations in Europe and beyond.

Farther south, the path of change is still uncertain. Though the 2005 defeat of the European constitution has apparently stalled EU enlargement, Romania, Bulgaria, and Croatia – as well as, most likely, Macedonia – have all built a more-or-less stable political system. All, though, have witnessed violent political turnover, or war, in 1989 or since; in all, ethnic divisions have more than once threatened to paralyze the country and may yet do so again. In all four cases, the borders of the nation are somewhat uncertain: the differences between a Romanian and a Moldovan, a Bulgarian and a Macedonian, a Croat and a Bosnian Croat are either insignificant or crucial, depending on one's perspective. None, however, has yet to examine seriously the past; in this sense, they are all farther removed from the ongoing transformation of Europe described above.

Peering into Serbia-Montenegro, Bosnia-Hercegovina, and Albania, we are at the edge of Europe's Black Hole. To continue the metaphor, it is not clear whether these three will escape. In 2005, Albania held a parliamentary election that brought a change in government – former President Sali Berisha reclaiming power from his archrival Fatos Nano, who reluctantly acknowledged defeat.

In Serbia, the political determination that followed the Djindjić assassination quickly dissipated. Perhaps the exorcism of Serbia's demons will begin with Slobodan Milošević's death. Yet the country is at any rate likely to fall into three parts with a few years, as both Montenegro (the last of the Yugoslav republics without independence) and Kosovo secede, with EU approval. In Bosnia-Hercegovina, it is not yet certain if there is a state, or simply a protectorate of the European Union. This last case remains a test of the value of foreign intervention in bringing about stability and democracy. A decade after the Dayton Accords, Bosnia may not yet have begun the process of transformation that other countries began in the 1980s.

This cautious survey underscores the impermanence of the region itself. The end of the post-communist era in parts of Eastern Europe raises once again a question that emerged first in the early 1990s: How do we know which countries are in fact on a path toward economic and political change, and which ones are (now, or for the long term) incapable of such change? The success of some countries that had little or no experience with democracy or the protection of human rights before 1989 suggests that change is more plausible than it seems. What, then, of the nations farther east? Are Ukraine, Belarus, and Moldova, for example, part of the Eastern Europe described here? The question is not a geographic one – fifteen countries is plenty for one regional story – but a political one. Are the same processes occurring across the next swath of countries, or do they simply belong to a different story altogether?

The Orange Revolution in Kyiv in November – December 2004, in which massive street protests forced a re-running of the presidential election, followed by a dramatic reorientation of the country toward the entire agenda previously embraced by Ukraine's Western neighbors, shows that Ukraine has hopes of becoming a part of the Eastern Europe described here. The Orange Revolution was a proud descendant of the Otpor Revolution in Serbia (by way of the Rose Revolution in Georgia in 2003), as well as of 1989 itself. Moldova, which is no more in control of its territory than was Croatia in 1993 (the east is controlled by a Russian-supported secessionist group), and Belarus, under the rule of the last true authoritarian dictator in Europe, may not be so lucky. Their post-communist era may yet be far ahead.

One of the frequent complaints about NATO and EU expansion is that, as it moves across Eastern Europe, it simply replicates the Iron Curtain of old, placing a new barrier farther to the east, thus excluding these and other countries. But this new curtain is hardly as solid as the one it succeeded. Neither side is determined to use force to keep its citizens in. Nor, without some rather absurd semantics, can one say that the division is ideologically defined. Indeed, the line that separates the EU from countries to the East has a provisional quality to it: even if expansion is not really in the works, the conversation about expansion continues.

The border is just as fuzzy to the West. Eastern Europe is a New Europe, shaped by its communist and dissident past, and by the legacies of a century of ethnic cleansing. New Europe, though, is no longer the "lands between," sandwiched between imperial powers and ideological enemies, as an old history of the region described it. As the people of this New Europe have grappled with their national pasts (or refused to do so), engaged in destructive civil wars, and articulated their own ideas of what it means to be European, they have changed the Old Europe as much as it has changed them. The shock, in the post-communist era, has been mutual.

Notes

Introduction: the shock of the new

1 Milan Kundera (1929–), Danilo Kiš (1935–89), and Czesław Miłosz (1911–2004) are writers from Czechoslovakia, Yugoslavia, and Poland, respectively.

2 European Commission, *Eurobarometer 2004.1: Public Opinion in the Candidate Countries*. Available at <europa.eu.int/comm/public_opinion>. See also "Change and Decay," *The Economist*, August 27, 2005, p. 58.

3 Quoted in Rachel Walker, *Six Years that Shook the World: Perestroika, the Impossible Project* (Manchester: Manchester University Press, 1993), p. 217.

4 There is no room here to discuss the social movements that contributed to the fall of communism. I refer the reader to my *A Carnival of Revolution: Central Europe, 1989* (Princeton, NJ: Princeton University Press, 2002).

5 See Michael D. Kennedy, "Contingencies and the Alternatives of 1989: Toward a Theory and Practice of Negotiating Revolution," *East European Politics and Societies*, 13: 2 (spring 1999), pp. 293–302.

6 Roland Breton, "Flag Resurrection in Eastern Europe," *The Flag Bulletin*, 137 (1990), pp. 174–87. Hungary's communist emblem had been removed from the flag after 1956, but the hole reappeared in 1989, as a memory of that uprising.

7 Slavenka Drakulić, *Café Europa: Life After Communism* (New York: Penguin, 1996), p. 4.

1 Different paths on an open road: economic and social change

1 See Gertrude E. Schroeder, "Economic Legacies of Communism: A Common Inheritance," in J. Serafin (ed.), *East-Central Europe in the 1990s* (Boulder, CO: Westview Press, 1994), pp. 57–78.

2 Ivan T. Berend, *Central and Eastern Europe 1944–1993: Detour from the Periphery to the Periphery* (Cambridge: Cambridge University Press, 1996), pp. 231.

3 Janine Wedel, *Collision and Collusion: The Strange Case of Western Aid to Eastern Europe* (New York: Palgrave, 2001), p. 210.

4 Robin Okey, *The Demise of Communist East Europe: 1989 in Context* (London: Arnold, 2004), pp. 118–19.

5 Wedel, *Collision and Collusion*, pp. 29–30.

6 Venelin I. Ganev, "The 'Triumph of Neoliberalism' Reconsidered: Critical Remarks on Ideas-Centered Analyses of Political and Economic Change in Post-Communism," *East European Politics and Societies*, 19: 3 (2005), esp. pp. 361 and 369.

7 Okey, *Demise of Communist East Europe*, p. 164.

8 Wedel, *Collision and Collusion*. Venelin Ganev, citing Wedel, casts doubts on the hegemony of neoliberal ideas in his "The 'Triumph of Neoliberalism' Reconsidered."

9 Andreas Beckmann, "Green Views: The Burden of Sisyphus?," *Transitions Online* [*TOL*], July 23, 2003.

10 Ben Fowkes, *The Post-Communist Era: Change and Continuity in Eastern Europe* (New York: St. Martin's Press, 1999), p. 136.

11 "Protracted Refugee Situations," Report of the United Nations High Commissioner for Refugees, June 10, 2004, at <www.unhcr.org/cgi-bin/texis/vtx/excom/opendoc.pdf?tbl=EXCOM&id=40ed5b384>.

12 Jean-Paul Sardon, "Demographic Change in the Balkans Since the End of the 1980s," *Population: An English Selection*, 13: 2 (2001), pp. 49–70.

13 Data available at <epp.eurostat.cec.eu.int>.

14 András Blahó, "Social Transformation in Four Central European Countries: 1989–2003," *Transition Studies Review*, 11: 3 (2004), pp. 127–57; Michael F. Förster, David Jesuit, and Timothy M. Smeeding, *Regional Poverty and Income Inequality in Central and Eastern Europe: Evidence from the Luxembourg Income Study*, Discussion Paper 2003/65 (Helsinki: United Nations University, World Institute for Development Economics Research, 2003).

15 Quoted in Mihai Sturdza, "The National Salvation Front and the Workers," *Report on Eastern Europe*, 1: 25 (June 22, 1990), p. 31.

16 Michael Shafir, "Government Encourages Vigilant Violence in Bucharest," *Report on Eastern Europe*, 1: 27 (July 6, 1990), p. 33.

17 Grzegorz Ekiert and Jan Kubik, *Rebellious Civil Society: Popular Protest and Democratic Consolidation in Poland, 1989–1993* (Ann Arbor: University of Michigan Press, 1999), p. 112.

18 The term is from Mitchell A. Orenstein, *Out of the Red: Building Capitalism and Democracy in Postcommunist Europe* (Ann Arbor: University of Michigan Press, 2001), ch. 5.

19 See Stephen Crowley and David Ost, "Introduction: The Surprise of Labor Weakness in Postcommunist Society," in S. Crowley and D. Ost (eds), *Workers After Workers' States: Labor and Politics in Postcommunist Eastern Europe* (Lanham, MD: Rowman and Littlefield, 2001), p. 8.

20 Miklós Haraszti, *The Velvet Prison: Artists Under State Socialism* (New York: Noonday Press, 1987).

21 Sardon, "Demographic Change in the Balkans," p. 55.

22 I am indebted to Elizabeth Dunn for this observation.

23 Gail Kligman and Stephanie Limoncelli, "Trafficking Women After Socialism: To, Through, and From Eastern Europe," *Social Politics*, 12: 1 (spring 2005), pp. 118–40.

24 Geoffrey D. Gooch, "Environmental Beliefs and Attitudes in Sweden and the Baltic States," *Environment and Behavior*, 27: 4 (July 1995), pp. 513–39.

25 Elizabeth C. Dunn, *Privatizing Poland: Baby Food, Big Business, and the Remaking of Labor* (Ithaca, NY: Cornell University Press, 2004), pp. 119–25.

26 János István Tóth and Endre Sik, "Hidden Economy in Hungary 1992–1999," in R. Neef and M. Stanculescu (eds), *The Social Impact of Informal Economies in Eastern Europe* (Burlington, VT: Ashgate, 2002), p. 221; Constantin Ciupagea, "Economic Functions of Informal Activities in Romania," in ibid., p. 191.

27 See Deema Kaneff, "The Shame and Pride of Market Activity: Morality, Identity and Trading in Postsocialist Rural Bulgaria," in R. Mandel and C. Humphrey (eds), *Markets and Moralities: Ethnographies of Postsocialism* (Oxford and New York: Berg, 2002), pp. 33–51.

28 See Galen Spencer Hull, *Small Businesses Trickling Up in Central and Eastern Europe* (New York and London: Garland, 1999).

29 Matloob Piracha and Roger Vickermann, "Immigration, Labour Mobility, and EU Enlargement," in J. Smith and C. Jenkins (eds), *Through the Paper Curtain: Insiders and Outsiders in the New Europe* (London: Blackwell, 2003), pp. 42–3.

30 Ibid., pp. 42, 47.

31 Jan Skórzyński, *Ugoda i rewolucja. Władza i opozycja, 1985–1989* (Warsaw: Rzeczpospolita, 1995), p. 132.

2 In praise of ethnic cleansing? National struggles

1 Dumitru Balaci, "Notes from Bucharest: Burying the King – and Kings," *Transitions Online*, February 26, 2003.

2 Rada Nikolaev, "The Public Debate over Restoring the Monarchy," *Report on Eastern Europe*, 2: 27 (July 5, 1991), p. 4.

3 Vladimir Tismaneanu, *Fantasies of Salvation: Democracy, Nationalism, and Myth in Post-Communist Europe* (Princeton, NJ: Princeton University Press, 1998), pp. 42–3.

4 Tismaneanu, *Fantasies of Salvation*, p. 108.

5 Jiri Pehe, "The Czech Republic," *RFE/RL Research Report,* 3: 16 (April 22, 1994), p. 53.

6 See Paul Hockenos, *Free to Hate: The Rise of the Right in Post-Communist Eastern Europe* (New York: Routledge, 1993), ch. 1.

7 Jonathan Kaufman, *A Hole in the Heart of the World: The Jewish Experience in Eastern Europe after World War II* (New York: Penguin, 1997), p. 261.

8 Janine P. Holc, "Memory Contested: Jewish and Catholic Views of Auschwitz in Present-Day Poland," in Robert Blobaum (ed.), *Antisemitism*

and Its Opponents in Modern Poland (Ithaca, NY and London: Cornell University Press, 2005), p. 317.

9 David J. Smith, *Estonia: Independence and European Integration* (New York: Routledge, 2001), p. 88.

10 Greg Nieuwsma, "A Depressing Decade: Czech–Roma Relations After the Velvet Revolution," *Central Europe Review*, 1: 18 (October 25, 1999), available at <www.tol.cz>.

11 The remark has been reported in many different ways; Louis Sell reports that it may actually have been only an order to the police to stop using truncheons. Nevertheless, it became legend, and inspired subsequent Serb national campaigns. Louis Sell, *Slobodan Milošević and the Destruction of Yugoslavia* (Durham, NC: Duke University Press, 2002), pp. 1–2.

12 Laura Silber and Allan Little, *Yugoslavia: Death of a Nation*, rev. edn (New York: Penguin, 1997), pp. 154–8.

13 Ibid., p. 215.

14 On rape and partition, see Robert M. Hayden, "Rape and Rape Avoidance in Ethno-National Conflicts: Sexual Violence in Liminalized States," *American Anthropologist*, 102: 1 (2000), pp. 27–41.

15 J. F. Brown, *The Grooves of Change: Eastern Europe at the Turn of the Millennium* (Durham, NC: Duke University Press, 2001), p. 174.

16 Karen Henderson, *Slovakia: The Escape from Invisibility* (New York: Routledge, 2002), p. 36.

17 Peter Martin, "Economic Reform and Slovakia," *Report on Eastern Europe* 2: 27 (July 5, 1991), p. 8.

18 Shari J. Cohen, *Politics without a Past: The Absence of History in Postcommunist Nationalism* (Durham, NC: Duke University Press, 1999), p. 129.

19 Michael J. Deis, "A Study of Nationalism in Czechoslovakia," *RFE/RL Research Report*, 1: 5 (January 31, 1992), pp. 9, 12.

20 Hugh Poulton, *Who are the Macedonians?* 2nd edn (Bloomington: Indiana University Press, 2000), pp. 214–15.

21 Henryk J. Sokalski, *An Ounce of Prevention: Macedonia and the UN Experience in Preventive Diplomacy* (Washington, DC: United States Institute of Peace Press, 2003).

3 Peeling away the past: nostalgia and punishment

1 See Max Paul Friedman and Padraic Kenney, "Introduction," in M. P. Friedman and P. Kenney (eds), *Partisan Histories: The Past in Contemporary Global Politics* (New York: Palgrave, 2005), pp. 1–14.

2 Jacek Żakowski, *Rewanż pamięci* (Warsaw: sic!, 2002).

3 Quoted in "Founded on War Crimes?", *TOL*, May 16, 2005.

4 Gary Jonathan Bass, *Stay the Hand of Vengeance: The Politics of War Crimes Tribunals* (Princeton, NJ: Princeton University Press, 2000), p. 215.

5 Miklos Haraszti, "Hungary: Decade of the Handshake Transition," *TOL*, January 15, 1999.

6 RFE/RL Newsline, 3: 28, part 2, February 10, 1999. Available at <www. rferl.org>.

7 Vaclav Havel, "New Year's Day Speech, 1990," in G. Stokes (ed.), *From Stalinism to Pluralism: A Documentary History of Eastern Europe Since 1945*, 2nd edn (New York and Oxford: Oxford University Press, 1996), p. 250.

8 Tina Rosenberg, *The Haunted Land: Facing Europe's Ghosts After Communism* (New York: Vintage, 1996), p. 89.

9 Lawrence Weschler, "The Velvet Purge: The Trials of Jan Kavan," *The New Yorker*, October 19, 1992, pp. 66–96.

10 Weschler, quoting Kavan, in ibid., p. 72; Rosenberg, *The Haunted Land*, p. 109.

11 Quoted in Noel Calhoun, *Dilemmas of Justice in Eastern Europe's Democratic Transitions* (New York: Palgrave, 2004), p. 123.

12 Louis Zanga, "Albania's Former President Remains Unrepentant," *RFE/RL Research Report*, 3: 29 (July 22, 1994), p. 12.

13 T. D. Whipple (ed.), *After the Velvet Revolution: Václav Havel and the New Leaders of Czechoslovakia Speak Out* (New York: Freedom House, 1991), pp. 134–5.

14 Anne Applebaum, "The Three Lives of Helena Brus," *Sunday Telegraph*, December 6, 1998. Available at <www.anneapplebaum.com>.

15 *Szoborpark Muzeum Budapest* (Budapest: Akos Rethly, n.d.).

16 Dan Ionescu, "Marshal Ion Antonescu Honored by Old and New Admirers," *Report on Eastern Europe*, 1: 34 (August 24, 1990), p. 37.

17 Michael Shafir, "Memory, Memorials, and Membership: Romanian Utilitarian Anti-Semitism and Marshal Antonescu," in W. Moskovich, O. Luthar, and I. Šumi (eds), *Jews and Anti-Semitism in the Balkans* (Jerusalem and Ljubljana: Hebrew University of Jerusalem, Center for Slavic Languages and Literatures, 2004), pp. 121–4.

18 Shari J. Cohen, *Politics without a Past: The Absence of History in Postcommunist Nationalism* (Durham, NC: Duke University Press, 1999), pp. 146–50.

19 Jan Tomasz Gross, *Neighbors: The Destruction of the Jewish Community in Jedwabne, Poland* (Princeton, NJ: Princeton University Press, 2001). Some of the discussion generated by the book's earlier Polish edition is reprinted in Antony Polonsky and Joanna B. Michlic (eds), *The Neighbors Respond: The Controversy Over the Jedwabne Massacre in Poland* (Princeton, NJ: Princeton University Press, 2004).

20 Padraic Kenney, "Martyrs and Neighbors: Sources of Reconciliation in Central Europe," *Common Knowledge* (forthcoming, 2006).

21 Ibid.

22 Karoly Okolocsanyi, "Hungarian Compensation off to a Slow Start," *RFE/RL Research Report*, 2: 11 (March 12, 1993), p. 52.

23 Joan Lofgren, "Estonia Rectifies Its Past, Complicates Its Present," *Transition* 2: 2 (January 26, 1996), p. 28.

24 Tony Judt, "The Past is Another Country: Myth and Memory in Postwar Europe," in I. Deak, J. Gross, and T. Judt (eds), *The Politics of Retribution in Europe: World War II and Its Aftermath* (Princeton, NJ: Princeton University Press, 2000), p. 307.

25 Peeter Sauter, "Czy Lenin żyje," in F. Modrzejewski and M. Sznajderman (eds), *Nostalgia. Eseje o tęsknocie za komunizmem* (Wołowiec: Czarne, 2002), p. 87.

4 Portraits of hubris: democratic politics

1 Václav Havel, "New Year's Day Speech, 1990," in G. Stokes (ed.), *From Stalinism to Pluralism: A Documentary History of Eastern Europe Since 1945*, 2nd edn (New York: Oxford University Press, 1996), pp. 250, 252, 253.

2 <www.freedomhouse.org>.

3 Louisa Vinton, "Walesa, 'Special Powers,' and the Balcerowicz Plan," *Report on Eastern Europe*, 2: 29 (July 19, 1991), p. 16; Mitchell A. Orenstein, *Out of the Red: Building Capitalism and Democracy in Postcommunist Europe* (Ann Arbor: University of Michigan Press, 1999), pp. 32–3.

4 Kjell Engelbrekt, "The Union of Democratic Forces Consolidates Before June Election," *Report on Eastern Europe*, 1: 22 (June 1, 1990).

5 Anna M. Grzymała-Busse, *Redeeming the Communist Past: The Regeneration of Communist Parties in East Central Europe* (Cambridge: Cambridge University Press, 2002), pp. 103–4.

6 Louisa Vinton, "Poland's Political Spectrum on the Eve of the Elections," *RFE/RL Research Report*, 2: 36 (September 10, 1993), p. 6.

7 Grzymała-Busse, *Redeeming the Communist Past*, p. 210.

8 Quoted in Abby Innes, *Czechoslovakia: The Short Goodbye* (New Haven, CT: Yale University Press, 2001), p. 244.

9 Louis Sell, *Slobodan Milosevic and the Destruction of Yugoslavia* (Durham, NC: Duke University Press, 2002), p. 132.

10 Laura Secor, "Rage Against the Regime: Serbian Students Fight Milosevic," *Lingua Franca* (September 2000), pp. 43, 40.

11 See Samuel Huntington, *The Clash of Civilizations and the Remaking of World Order* (New York: Simon and Schuster, 1996), esp. pp. 52–3, 192–4.

12 Jeffrey S. Kopstein and David A. Reilly, "Geographic Diffusion and the Transformation of the Postcommunist World," *World Politics*, 53: 1 (October 2000), pp. 1–37.

13 Lawrence Weschler, "Letter from Serbia: Aristotle in Belgrade," *The New Yorker*, February 10, 1997, pp. 33, 35.

14 Slavenka Drakulić, *The Balkan Express: Fragments from the Other Side of the War* (New York: HarperCollins, 1994); Dubravka Ugrešić, *The Culture of Lies: Antipolitical Essays* (University Park, PA: Pennsylvania State University Press, 1998).

15 I am indebted to Jacek Lubecki for this discussion. See his "Civic Traditions in Poland and Italy: A Comparative Study of Regional Political Cultures" (PhD diss., Denver University, 2000).

5 A new Europe: the East in the West

1 George H. W. Bush, in "The Wall Comes Down, 1989," Episode 23 in *The Cold War* (CNN Productions, 1998).

2 Jan Obrman, "Withdrawal of Soviet Troops Completed," *Report on Eastern Europe*, 2: 30 (July 26, 1991), p. 17; see also Alfred A. Reisch, "Free of Soviet Military Forces after Forty-Six Years," in ibid., pp. 21–32.

3 Obrman, "Withdrawal of Soviet Troops Completed," p. 17.

4 Available at <old/hrad.cz/president/Havel/speeches/1990/2102_uk.html>.

5 Timothy Snyder, *The Reconstruction of Nations: Poland, Ukraine, Lithuania, Belarus, 1569–1999* (New Haven, CT: Yale University Press, 2003), p. 236.

6 Zoltan Barany, "Visegrad Four Contemplate Separate Paths," *Transition*, 1: 14 (August 11, 1995), p. 58.

7 Ivan Drach, quoted in Snyder, *The Reconstruction of Nations*, p. 263.

8 Quoted in J.F. Brown, *The Grooves of Change: Eastern Europe at the Turn of the Millennium* (Durham, NC: Duke University Press, 2001), p. 218.

9 Quoted in Stanley Kober, "The United States and the Enlargement Debate," *Transition*, 1: 23 (December 15, 1995), p. 7.

10 On NATO attitudes toward expansion, see Ronald D. Asmus, *Opening NATO's Door: How the Alliance Remade Itself for a New Era* (New York: Columbia University Press, 2002).

11 Laura Silber and Allan Little, *Yugoslavia: Death of a Nation*, rev. edn (New York: Penguin, 1997), pp. 150–1.

12 Quoted in ibid., p. 159.

13 Sabrina Ramet, *Balkan Babel: The Disintegration of Yugoslavia from the Death of Tito to the Fall of Milošević*, 4th edn (Boulder, CO: Westview Press, 2002), pp. 178–9.

14 Asmus, *Opening NATO's Door*, p. 125; Troop estimates as of November 1994 (by which time the Czech Republic and Slovakia had separated): <www.un.org/Depts/DPKO/Missions/unprof_b.htm>.

15 See Dimitrij Rupel, "Slovenia's Shift from the Balkans to Central Europe," in J. Benderly and E. Kraft (eds), *Independent Slovenia: Origins, Movements, Prospects* (New York: St. Martin's Press, 1994), pp. 183–200.

16 Samantha Power, *"A Problem from Hell": America and the Age of Genocide* (New York: HarperCollins, 2002).

17 Silber and Little, *Yugoslavia*, p. 247.

18 Jan Willem Honig and Norbert Both, *Srebrenica: Record of a War Crime* (New York: Penguin, 1996), p. 148.

19 Thierry Domin, "PLIP and DPREs: The Figures for 2002," available at <www.nato.int/sfor/indexinf/158/p12a/t02p12a.htm>.

20 "New Figures on Civilian Deaths in Kosovo War," Human Rights Watch Report, February, 2000. <www.hrw.org/press/2000/02/nato207.htm>.

21 See Connie Bruck, "The World According to Soros," *The New Yorker*, January 23, 1995, pp. 54–78; Michael T. Kaufman, *Soros: The Life and Times of a Messianic Billionaire* (New York: Knopf, 2002).

22 Malcolm Chalmers, "Spending to Save: Retrospective Case Studies," University of Bradford, Centre for International Cooperation and Security Working Paper 2, April 2005; for comparison, official development assistance to Romania, a comparably-sized country (albeit with negligible foreign debt in 1989) in the years 1990–2003 totalled 4.6 billion dollars. Data from <unstats.un.org>.

23 Quoted in Jan B. de Weydenthal, "EC Keeps Central Europe at Arm's Length," *RFE/RL Research Report*, 2: 5 (January 29, 1993), p. 29.

24 Karoly Okolicsany, "Eastern Views of the EBRD," *RFE/RL Research Report*, 2: 23 (June 4, 1993), p. 51.

25 Quoted in Peter A. Poole, *Europe Unites: The EU's Eastern Enlargement* (Westport, CT: Praeger, 2003), p. 38.

26 "Common Declaration of Pope John Paul II and His Beatitude Christopoulos," Athens, May 4, 2001, at <www.catholicculture.org/docs/doc_viewcfw?recnum=3570>.

27 See Kristi Raik, "EU Accession of Central and Eastern European Countries: Democracy and Integration as Conflicting Logics," *East European Politics and Societies*, 18: 4 (2004), p. 576.

28 "United We Stand," *Wall Street Journal*, January 30, 2003.

29 Christian Semler, "Die heiligen drei Könige und das Morgenland," *Die Tageszeitung*, March 8, 2003.

30 Adam Michnik, "My, zdrajcy," *Gazeta wyborcza*, March 29–30, 2003, pp. 10–11.

31 See Ronald D. Asmus and Alexandr Vondra, "The Origins of Atlanticism in Central and Eastern Europe," *Cambridge Review of International Affairs*, 18: 2 (July 2005), pp. 203–16; Jacek Lubecki, "Poland in Iraq: The Politics of the Decision," *Polish Review*, 50: 1 (2005), pp. 69–92.

32 Jürgen Habermas and Jacques Derrida, "February 15, or, What Binds Europeans Together: Pleas for a Common Foreign Policy, Beginning in Core Europe," and Adam Krzemiński, "First Kant, Now Habermas: A Polish Perspective on 'Core Europe,'" in D. Levy, M. Pensky, and J. Torpey (eds), *Old Europe, New Europe, Core Europe: Transatlantic Relations After the Iraq War* (London: Verso, 2005), pp. 4, 146–7. The essays originally appeared in the *Frankfurter Allgemeine Zeitung* and *Neue Zürcher Zeitung*, respectively.

33 Elaine Sciolino, "Caustic Turn Jolts Europe: Failed Talks at Summit Expose Union Problems," *The New York Times*, national edn, June 19, 2005, p. A1.

Index

acid rain, 27
Afghanistan, Russian invasion of, 5
agriculture, in European Union policy, 151–2
AIDS, 39
Albania, 7, 16, 29, 30, 46, 73, 74, 87, 89, 101, 102, 140, 158, 160; elections in, 104; standard of living in, 42
Albanian National Army, 74
Albright, Madeline, 137, 145
Alia, Ramiz, 87
Alliance of Free Democrats (Hungary), 104
Amnesty International, 75
Antall, József, 50–1, 94, 104, 106, 133
antisemitism, 53, 90, 94
antiwar demonstrations in Europe, 157
Antonescu, Ion, 92–3
Arbour, Louise, 78
Ashdown, Paddy, 117
Aspin, Les, 136
assassinations of political leaders, 122

Badinter Commission, 139
Baker, James, 129
Balcerowicz, Leszek, 20, 24
Baltic Republics, 54, 69, 102, 106, 108, 124, 129, 131; transition in, 23
Băsescu, Traian, 117
Bass, Gary, 78
Be Active, Be Emancipated (B.a.b.e.) (Croatia), 37

Belarus, 161, 162
Belka, Marek, 158
Berisha, Sali, 87, 160
Boban, Mate, 64, 65
Boross, Péter, 112
Bosnia-Hercegovina, 3, 7, 61–7, 72, 101, 117, 139, 141, 158, 160, 161; elections in, 104; returning Muslims stoned, 98
Bosnian war, 29, 56, 60, 96, 117, 140, 142–3; rape as weapon of war, 37, 64; refugees from, 42
brain drain, from Bulgaria, 36
Brazauskas, Algirdas, 110
Brezhnev doctrine, 5
Brus, Helena Wolińska, 90
Bujak, Zbigniew, 88
Bulgaria, 9, 16, 21, 47–8, 72, 107, 133, 134, 158, 160; and NATO, 144, 155; brain drain from, 36; debt of, 18; success of former communists in, 113; transition in, 21; Turkish minority in, 54
Bulgarian Agrarian National Union, 104
Bush, George H.W., 80, 129
Bush, George W., 154

Catholic Church, as property owner, 97
Ceauşescu, Elena, 9, 82
Ceauşescu, Nicolae, 9, 18, 33, 46, 49, 82, 86, 116; fall of, 102
Chamberlain, Neville, 141
Charter 77 (Czechoslovakia), 5, 8
Chernobyl reactor leak, 38
China, 46
Chirac, Jacques, 154

Christodoulos, Archbishop, 152
Christopher, Warren, 141
churches, role of, 29–30
citizen vouchers, 21
citizenship, reconsideration of,
43
Civic Democratic Party
(Czechoslovakia), 109
Civic Forum (Czechoslovakia),
108, 109
civil rights, 146, 147
civil society, 95; strength of, 32
class, loses mobilising force, 34
Clinton, Bill, 137, 140–1, 144, 146
Cold War, 75, 136
collaboration, 81, 83, 84, 85
Committee to Help the Poor
(Hungary), 5
communism: collapse of, 16, 19,
52, 75; expropriation under,
96; internationalism of, 46;
movement away from, 127;
nostalgia for, 41
communist leaders, prosecution
of, 86, 87
communist parties: confiscation
of property of, 97; land
holdings surrendered, 96;
return to power, 98
communist past: nostalgia for, 3,
75–99; punishing crimes of,
112
communist society: inability to
adapt, 4; mobility within, 3
communists, return of, 109–14
Constantinescu, Emil, 116
corruption, 40
Council for Mutual Economic
Assistance (CMEA/
COMECON), 17
Croatia, 3, 29, 30, 73, 76, 93, 94,
95, 96, 104, 106, 113, 114,
117–18, 125, 138, 140, 158,
160; and Iraq war, 156
Croatian Democratic Union, 126

Croatian language, use of, 64–5
Croatian Spring, 89
Croatian war, 56, 59–61
Csurka, István, 50, 112
Czech Republic, 95, 97, 113, 124,
133, 147, 154; compensation
problems in, 96–7; EU
membership of, 150; flooding
in, 30–1; foreign investment
in, 23; membership of NATO,
137, 144
Czechoslovakia, 6, 8, 16, 21, 22,
36, 46, 52, 83, 84, 88–9, 101–2,
105, 108–9, 123, 133, 160;
accession to EU, 148; break-up
of, 56, 115; Chamberlain's
view of, 141; dissolution of,
69–72; elections in, 104; Roma
people in (attacks on, 50;
settlement of, 55); Russian
invasion of, 5; Soviet troops in,
129, 130; transition in, 23;
troops in Bosnian war, 140;
Velvet Revolution, 8, 18, 102,
115

Dayton talks, 67, 68, 143, 144
debt: of Eastern European
countries, 18; Russian default,
31
democracy, 76, 87, 126; building
of, 146–7, 156; scaled rating of,
101
Democratic Party of Albanians, 74
democratic politics, 100–27
passim
democratization, 5, 75
demonstrations, 18, 32
Demszky, Gábor, 81
dialogue, as revolutionary
concept, 9
Diena newspaper, 159
Dienstbier, Jiří, 140
Dimitrov, Filip, 108
dissidents, 5, 81, 109, 124, 128,

140, 154–5; ambivalence towards, 108

Djindjić, Zoran, 119; assassination of, 122, 125, 161

Dlouhý, Vladimir, 149

Drakulić, Slavenka, 12, 125

Drasković, Vuk, 119

Dubček, Alexander, 70, 88

Dzurinda, Mikuláš, 116

East Germany, 6

Eastern Europe: barriers to European labour market, 151; cooperation with, 144, 148; emergence of new national entities, 76; identity shift in, 52; seen as backward, 141; terminology of, 1; viewed as different civilization, 123

economic activity, measurement of, 17

energy supplies, access to, 27

environmental issues, 26–7, 28, 39, 159

Eris, Irena, 41

Estonia, 54, 97, 113; and Iraq war, 156; EU membership of, 150

ethnic cleansing, 60–69,135, 137, 139, 141, 145, 146, 156

ethnopolitics, opposition to, 126

European Bank for Reconstruction and Development (EBRD), 149

European Parliament, 51

European Union (EU), 12, 60, 62, 160; accession to, 1, 11, 23, 26, 27, 29, 43, 70, 76, 80, 81, 127, 137, 138, 147–8, 159 (referenda on, 152); bureaucracy of, 153; constitution, failure of, 158; enlargement of, 2, 3, 42, 43, 153, 157, 162 (grounded in security issue, 157–8); forces in Bosnia, 67; Yugoslav conflict as a test case, 138–9

feminism, 38

Feral Tribune (Croatia), 118

Fidesz party (Hungary), 86

foreign consultants, influx of, 41

foreign direct investment, inflow of, 23

foreign ownership of property, restrictions on, 22

Former Yugoslav Republic of Macedonia (FYROM), 73

Forza Italia, 115

Freedom and Peace Movement (Poland), 6

Freedom House, 101

freedom of religious worship, 113

Funar, Gheorghe, 49

Garton Ash, Timothy, 8

Gebert, Konstanty, 67

gender studies programs, 37

genocide, 63, 66

Gerasimov, Gennadii, 130

German minorities: in Czechoslovakia, 97 (killing of, 95); in Eastern Europe, 53–4, 108

German unification, 28, 130, 131, 136, 137, 157

Gierek, Edward, 46, 98

glasnost, 5

Glemp, Józef, 53

Gligorov, Kiro, 73, 106; attempted assassination of, 122

Goldstone, Richard, 78

Göncz, Arpád, 105–6, 109

Gorbachev, Mikhail, 4–5, 8, 16, 58, 69, 80, 130, 136

Gotovina, Ante, 76–7

green issues, 38, 39

Gross, Jan, 94

Habermas, Jürgen, 157

Habsburg, Archduke Otto von, 47

Habsburg Empire, 70

happenings, 120

Haradinaj, Ramush, 77–8;
indictment of, 146
Hárai, Zsigmond, 86
Haraszti, Miklós, 36, 128
Havel, Václav, 8, 50, 70, 71, 80, 82,
83, 100, 101–2, 105, 108–9,
123, 154; loss of popularity, 81;
speech to US Congress, 132
Helsinki Accords, 75
Helsinki Citizens' Assembly, 103
Hercegovina, 64
Hohenzollern, Prince Paul, 48
Holbrooke, Richard, 66, 137
Holocaust, 52, 63, 76, 92, 99, 117,
145; compensation for victims
of, 96; complicity in, 94;
examination of, 75; prosecution of perpetrators, 90
Horn, Gyula, 112
House of Terror, Budapest, 90–1
housing: problem of apartment
blocks, 28; shortage of, 3
Howard, Michael, 136
Hoxha, Enver, 87
human rights: movements for,
121; standards of, 95
Hungarian Democratic Forum
(HDF), 50, 104
Hungarian Socialist Party, 112
Hungary, 4, 6, 8, 16, 27, 36, 49, 70,
80, 81, 94, 101, 102, 105–6,
113, 118, 121, 124, 128, 133,
134, 140, 147, 154, 160; 1956
revolution, 6, 11, 90, 112, 132;
accession to EU, 148, 150; as
puppet state of Nazi Germany,
92; debt of, 18; elections in,
103–4; foreign investment in,
23, 25; hidden economy in, 40;
membership of NATO, 137,
144; NATO troops in, 144;
Security Police, 90–1; Soviet
occupation of, 130–1; Soviet
troops in, 129; strikes in, 34;
transition in, 19, 20, 21, 23

Huntington, Samuel, 123
Husák, Gustáv, 9, 102

Iliescu, Ion, 50, 116, 126
illegal labor, 38
Implementation Force (IFOR),
143
independent economic activity,
40–1
Independent Smallholders
(Hungary), 104
industrial sector, 26
inflation, 20, 23, 24
informers under communism, 83
intelligentsia, effacing of, 36
Internal Macedonia Revolutionary
Organization – Democratic
Party of Macedonian National
Unity, 74
International Criminal Tribunal
for the Former Yugoslavia
(ICTY), 77, 78–9; model for war
crimes tribunal, 78
investment, foreign, 41
Iraq: embargo of, 18; failure of
reconstruction, 160; invasion
of Kuwait, 18; war, 128–9, 154,
157
Islam, 30, 65, 66; conversion to,
61
Izetbegović, Alija, 62, 66, 106

Jaruzelski, Wojciech, 6, 8, 87–8,
105
Jasenovac concentration camp,
94
Jedwabne (Poland), murder of
Jews, 94, 99
Jews, 62, 91; alleged conspiracy
of, 49, 50; elimination of, in
Holocaust, 52; expropriation
of, 97; expulsion of, 52; in
Hungary, 53; in Romania, 92;
loss of property of, 96;
murdered in Jedwabne

(Poland), 94, 99; renaissance of Jewish culture, 53; Slovak, deportation of, 93 *see also* antisemitism
Jiu Valley (Romania), mine closures in, 125
John Paul II, visits to Eastern Europe, 152

Kádár, János, 46, 112
Kaplan, Robert, *Balkan Ghosts*, 140–1
Karadzić, Radovan, 62, 65, 78, 143
Kaufman, Jonathan, 53
Kavan, Jan, 83–4
Keraterm concentration camp, 63
Klaus, Václav, 21, 71, 109, 133, 152
ključ system (Yugoslavia), 62
Koženy, Viktor, 21
Kohl, Helmut, 60, 130
Konrad, György, 154
Kosovo, 3, 67–8, 73, 77–8, 101, 145, 158, 161; bombing of, 146; war in, 68, 144–6; war refugees from, 29
Kosovo Liberation Army (KLA), 68, 73, 77
Kostunica, Vojislav, 121, 122
Kováč, Michal, 115, 116
Kováč Jr, Michal, abduction of, 115
Kožený, Victor, 21
Krajina, 60, 61, 118; ethnic cleansing in, 64; liberation of, 77
Krzemiński, Adam, 157
Kučan, Milan, 58–9, 104, 106, 109
Kundera, Milan, *The Joke*, 46
Kurón, Jacek, 34, 35
Kwaśniewski, Aleksander, 94, 111

Landsbergis, Vytautas, 106, 110
Latvia, 11, 54, 113, 139; accession to EU, 159

Le Meridien hotel, Budapest, 128
Le Pen, Jean-Marie, 45, 51
League of Communists (Slovenia), 57, 58
"Letter of Eight", 154
Lithuania, 21, 54, 69, 110, 139; accession to EU, 28; relations with Poland, 135; transition in, 23
Lukanov, Andrei, assassination of, 122
Luković, Milorad, 122
lustration, 82–6, 108, 109

Maastricht, Treaty of, 150
Macedonia, 7, 29, 72–4, 101, 106, 134, 139, 146, 158, 160; elections in, 104; ethnic violence in, 72–4; success of former communists in, 113
Macierewicz, Antoni, 85
majority-ethnicity parties, 126
malnutrition, among children, 28
market economy, 15, 16
Marković, Ante, 23, 24
Marshall Plan, 22; second, 19
Marxism, rejection of, 5
Marxism-Leninism, exhaustion of, 4
Masaryk, Tomáš, 70, 100, 123
Mazowiecki, Tadeusz, 8, 82, 85, 103, 107, 140
Mečiar, Vladimír, 71, 93, 115–16, 151
Medgyessy, Péter, 86, 99, 154
media, independent, 121
Memorial group (Russia), 92
memory, shortage of, 98
Mesić, Stipe, 118
Michael of Romania, King, 47–8, 93
Michnik, Adam, 128, 154, 155, 156
migrants, to EU countries, 42
migration, 25
Miller, Leszek, 154

Milošević, Mirjana, 119
Milošević, Slobodan, 33, 56–7, 58,
  59, 62, 66, 67, 68, 69, 86, 93,
  106, 114, 117, 118–21, 122,
  124, 125, 133, 138, 139, 145,
  146, 161; trial of, 78–9
miners, in Romania, 125
minorities, 53, 133, 134; and
  democracy, 147; Muslim, 134
  see also German; Jews; Roma;
  Turkish; Russian
Miodowicz, Alfred, 43
Mladenov, Petar, 105
Mladić, Ratko, 65–6, 78
Mladina magazine (Slovenia), 57
mobility, social, 42
Moldova, 161
monarchism, 47–8
Montenegro, 161
Mostar, bridge of, 65, 99
Mothers Against War
  (Yugoslavia), 37
Movement for a Democratic
  Slovakia (MDS), 115
Movement for Rights and
  Freedoms (Bulgaria), 54, 108
multi-ethnicity, as desired
  feature, 147

Nagy, Imre, 11
Nano, Fatos, 87, 160
nation states, 52; legitimacy of, 79
nation-building, 12, 144–53
national liberation, theme of, 10
National Salvation Front
  (Romania), 24, 33, 104, 116
national self-determination,
  concept of, 56, 63, 138–9
national symbols, choice of, 107
nationalism, 45–74 passim;
  regional, 10
negotiation: as part of transition,
  9; importance of, 7
New Europe, 128–9, 153–8
nomenklaturization, 22

Non-Aligned Movement, 46
North Atlantic Treaty
  Organization (NATO), 74, 80,
  142; bombing of Belgrade, 120;
  expansion of, 135–7, 138, 144,
  162; membership of, 134, 137
nostalgia for communist past,
  98–9
nuclear energy, 27, 28

Oleksy, Józef, 111
Olszewski, Jan, 107
Omarska concentration camp, 63
Orbán, Viktor, 80, 81, 90, 133
Otpor (Resistance) movement,
  Serbia, 120, 121, 161

Partnership for Peace, 144
Party of Romanian National
  Unity, 49
Pavelić, Ante, 93, 94
perestroika, 5
Pithart, Petr, 131
pluralism, as revolutionary
  concept, 9
Podkrepa movement (Bulgaria), 35
Poland, 4, 11, 16, 18, 21, 30, 52,
  84, 98, 101, 102, 107, 110–11,
  113, 121, 124, 133, 134–5, 147,
  154, 158, 160; accession to EU,
  148, 150; and Iraq war, 156;
  and NATO, 155; concern for
  anniversaries, 80; debt of, 18;
  effects of Solidarity movement
  in, 7–8; flooding in, 30–1;
  foreign investment in, 23;
  German minority in, 53–4;
  membership of NATO, 137,
  144; national identity of, 95;
  pyramid schemes in, 30; re-
  examination of history, 95;
  relations with Lithuania, 135;
  relative freedom of, 88; Soviet
  policy towards, 130; Soviet
  troops in, 131; strikes in, 34;

transition in, 19, 20, 23; troops in Bosnian war, 140
Polish and Hungarian Assistance for the Reconstruction of Europe (PHARE), 148–9
"Polish plumbers", 12, 151
Poos, Jacques, 138
post-communist era, 2
poverty, cycle of, 28–9
Prague Spring, 6, 84, 89, 130, 132
private property, 124
privatization, 20, 21, 22, 24, 25, 41
Public Against Violence group (Slovakia), 71
pyramid schemes, 30, 33

Račak massacre (Kosovo), 68
Radio Free Europe, 99, 116
Rakowski, Mieczys³aw, 19, 23
Rambouillet negotiations, 145–6
rape, as weapon of war, 37, 38, 64
Raznatović, Želijko "Arkan", assassination of, 122
refugees, 26, 29, 142; economic, 42; from Yugoslav wars, 73; recovery of homes, 143
restitution of property, 96
revolution, as term for events of 1989, 9
Riga, museum, 79
Roma: in Romania, 92; treatment of, 31, 55, 72 (killing of, 50; pogroms against, 55)
Roman, Petre, 49
Romania, 7, 16, 24, 33, 38, 52, 82, 89, 94, 95, 104, 114, 116–17, 125, 126, 158, 160; and NATO, 155; as puppet state of Nazi Germany, 92; as source for adoption of children, 40; debt of, 18; membership of NATO, 144; pyramid schemes in, 30; standard of living in, 42; success of former communists in, 113

Rugova, Ibrahim, 67
Ruml, Jiří, 83
Rumsfeld, Donald, 128
Rupel, Dimitrij, 140
Russia, 1, 158; demand for Polish land corridor, 132
Russian minorities, 53, 54–5, 69

Sachs, Jeffrey, 20
Šahovnica flag (Croatia), 60
Sąjūdis Movement for Reform (Lithuania), 106, 110
Sanader, Ivo, 77, 126
Sarajevo: shelling of, 142; war in, 63
Sauter, Peeter, 99
Scott, Brian, 51
Semler, Christian, 154
Serbia, 7, 24, 79, 96, 114, 118–21, 124–5, 145, 158, 160, 161; and Iraq war, 156; Greater, concept of, 58, 66, 67, 139 (end of, 119); transition in, 26
sex industry, 38
Silesia, 54; "Black Triangle", 27
Saxecoburggotski, Simeon (Tsar Simeon II), 47–8
Sládek, Miroslav, 50
Slovakia, 3, 27, 70, 71–2, 93, 94, 114–15, 117, 124, 151; membership of NATO, 144; tax system in, 31; transition in, 26
Slovenia, 41, 57, 106, 124, 138, 147; and Iraq war, 156; EU membership of, 150; membership of NATO, 144; success of former communists in, 113; transition in, 21, 23
smuggling, 40
Snyder, Timothy, 132
Social Democratic Party of the Republic of Poland, 110–11
social movements, emergence of, 32
Sokalski, Henryk, 74

Solidarity movement (Poland), 6, 35, 36, 87, 95, 105, 108, 110, 111; decline of, 107; election victory of, 7–8
Soros, George, 146
South Africa, reconciliation process in, 91–2
sovereignty, loss of, 152–3
Srebrenica, 140; genocide, 65–6, 125, 142; Muslim rising in, 61; UN troops involved at, 142
Stabilization Force (SFOR), 143
Stalinism, 92; purges, 84, 89–90
Stambolić, Ivan, 121; assassination of, 122
standard of living, rise in, 31
strikes, 32, 35; general, in Czechoslovakia, 18; in Hungary, 34; in Poland, 34
student protests, 105
Sudetenland, 55, 97
"suitcase trade", 39
Szoborpark, Budapest, 91

taxation, 31, 40
Thatcher, Margaret, 21, 80
"third way", search for, 16–17
Tiananmen Square massacre, 7
Tismaneanu, Vladimir, 49
Tiso, Jozef, 93
Tito, Josip, 10, 46, 52, 57, 98
Torgyán, József, 112
trade unions: communist, 36; disintegration of, 35; state-sponsored, 35
trafficking in women and children, 38
Trenchev, Konstantin, 35
Trianon, Treaty of, 133
Truth and Reconciliation Commissions, 92
Tudjman, Franjo, 53, 60, 61, 62, 64, 66, 73, 76, 93, 94, 95–6, 104, 106, 117–18, 125, 133, 139, 140, 145

Tudor, Corneliu Vadim, 49, 117
Turkey, 134
Turkish minorities, 53, 54; Bulgarization of, 54, 86
Tutu, Desmond, 92
Tyminski, Stan, 107

Ugrešić, Dubravka, 125
Ukraine, 135; Orange Revolution, 135, 161; women workers from, 38
Union of Soviet Socialist Republics (USSR), 6, 46–7, 52, 69, 89; 1991 coup in, 83; break-up of, 18, 56, 132; troops stationed in Eastern Europe, 130 (withdrawal of, 132)
United Nations (UN), 78, 140; peacekeeping forces, 142 (complicit in ethnic cleansing, 64, 65–6, 142)
UN Protection Force (UNPROFOR), 140, 142
UNMIK peacekeeping force, 146
UNPREDEP force (Macedonia), 73–4
unemployment, 17, 20, 42
Union of Democratic Forces (Bulgaria), 107–8
United States of America (USA), 138, 145, 156, 157; alliance with, 160
Ústí nad Labem (Czech Republic), ghetto wall in, 55

Vance-Owen Plan, 141
Vilnius Group, 154
Visegrad group, 133
Vukovar: ethnic cleansing in, 64; siege of, 60

Wałęsa, Lech, 8, 35, 44, 80, 82, 103, 105, 109, 110, 111–12; loses election, 85
war crimes, 145

Wechsler, Lawrence, 124–5
Wedel, Janine, 19
Wilson, Woodrow, 56, 138–9
women's movements, 37
women's rights, 38
Workers' Defense Committee
  (Poland), 5

Yugoslav wars, 23, 37, 137–43;
  costs of, 147; importance to
  European nationalism, 144

Yugoslavia, 2, 4, 16, 19, 24, 46, 52,
  55, 56–68, 101, 102, 106;
  break-up of, 56; multi-ethnic
  constituency of, 57

Zachęta Gallery, Warsaw, 98
Zajedno (Together) movement
  (Serbia), 119
Zhelev, Zhelyu, 105, 107–8
Zhivkov, Todor, 9, 46, 54, 86–7,
  134; fall of, 102